There aren't many books that lift your spirit at the same time they are breaking your heart, but that's just what Heather Gordon-Young accomplishes in her book, *Fireflies*. Her lyrical prose makes almost bearable the story of all-too-human suffering she encounters as she searches for Divine deliverance. What she discovers—and this is what makes *Fireflies* essential and unforgettable—is that it is in the very muck of human suffering and imperfection that the greatest transcendence can be found.

—Terry Wolverton, author of *Stealing Angel*

Heather Gordon-Young's *Fireflies* is a young woman's unflinchingly honest struggle to hold onto faith amid shadows and darkness. This narrative eschews easy ideas of what it means to be on a spiritual journey. Rather, Gordon-Young takes readers into the dark night of the soul, on an expedition of searching and stumbling and shouting. In doing so, she unearths a kind of illumination that is both tangible and fleeting, one that, while adding light to the scene, never attempts to deny the intensity of nightfall.

—Bernadette Murphy, author of the bestselling *Zen and the Art of Knitting: Exploring the Links Between Knitting, Spirituality, and Creativity*, among others. *Look, Lean, Roll: A Woman, A Motorcycle, and Plunging into Risk*, forthcoming Spring 2016

Candid and compelling, Heather's memoir is both spiritually insightful and stunningly written. Through the persistent darkness that gripped her family, she continued to find the "light in a dark world," the shining evidence of how God breaks through our hurt and doubt to deliver his perfect love and mercy. Heather's *Firefiles* is a burst of light into the dark room of our imperfect hearts; a compelling, tender account on mining for stones of hope in the depths of our past.

—Heather Luby, author of *Laws of Motion*, co-host of *Firsts in Fiction*

Heather Gordon-Young is a provocative narrator. Reminiscent of Anne Lamott, her nuanced voyage between sacred and secular culminates in her attempt to understand her brother's mental illness in *Fireflies: Finding Light in a Dark World*. Her crisp vocabulary as she upholds a "ministry of presence" for Jimmy, Charlie, Wendell, her father, and others peels back the layers of the underbelly of identity. Like the primordial core of the tree, Heather searches continents and finds an abiding understanding of hope, healing, and humility within the family. *Fireflies'* unique and timely commentary should become required reading in disciplines such as religious studies, sociology, and public health.

—Dr. Susanne Green, PhD

In *Fireflies: Finding Light in a Dark World*, Heather Gordon-Young has given us a beautifully written and unflinching work of faith, loss, and redemption. A luminous work of great clarity and courage.

—Andrew Todhunter, author of *A Meal Observed*

A powerful, inspirational read, this is a book about faith and family that eschews easy sentimentality for raw, immersive honesty. The account of one young woman's struggles to understand and help her brother who is battling a mental illness that has not been diagnosed is a necessary look at a broken mental health system. Told with lyrical language and a compelling storytelling style, *Fireflies* will grab you from the first pages and stay with you long after you've finished reading.

—Erica Moody, editor, *The Citron Review*

Fireflies depicts a rich coming of age in faith. Gordon-Young's quest for compassion, for "a better to way to be a human being" is rife with admirable tenderness and pluck. Here is a companion to, and from, the deep home place—and the lighted presence of those loved, divided, and divided in themselves.

—Donald Morrill, author of *The Untouched Minutes* and *Awaiting Your Impossibilities*

Prepare to read this book with your mouth open, shaking your head at Heather Gordon-Young's audacious, ever-questioning faith. When I finished her moving last chapter, I had no choice but to see my own faith and ability to love in a different light. Come boldly, indeed.

—LeVan D. Hawkins, author, poet, performer

With rich, almost poetic language, Heather Gordon-Young bravely and sensitively shares both ordinary and painful experiences and mystifying holy moments, experiences that cannot be explained with logic, only with the heart.

When confronted with a stranger instead of the person you know, witnessing a loved one in the midst of a psychotic episode can be a horrifying experience, but stories like Heather's must be told if we are to know the pain of serious mental illness and work for more compassionate churches and institutions.

—The Rev. Mary Janet "Bean" Murray

To be able to give a testimony, one has to have had a test. *Fireflies* by Heather Gordon-Young is an amazing example of such raw, heartfelt testimony of mental illness within a family. She unearths the dire need for the Church to be a hospital for the soul. So many souls have been lost, exposing a rift between the medical, spiritual, and religious fields of healing. Heather uses a paintbrush to express her words, filling the canvas with the raw expression of the dichotomy between spirituality and religiosity. It is clear that the command from Jesus to "preach the kingdom and heal the sick" (Luke 9:2) has, for the most part, been ignored today. Heather's search for healing and a cure within the Church offers a faint glimmer of hope. I urge you therefore to observe this "painting" through Heather's eyes as she battles the darkness of dis-ease within her own family and within the family of the Church. Read *Fireflies* and weep—better yet, reap the wisdom held within these pages.

—The Rev. Nigel W. D. Mumford, *By His Wounds Ministry*,
author of *Hand to Hand: From Combat to Healing*,
The Forgotten Touch: More Stories of Healing,
and *After the Trauma, the Battle Begins: Post Trauma Healing*

Fireflies

Finding Light
in a
Dark World

HEATHER GORDON-YOUNG

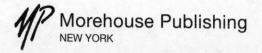 Morehouse Publishing
NEW YORK

For Jimmy

Morehouse Publishing, 19 East 34th Street, New York, NY 10016

Morehouse Publishing is an imprint of Church Publishing Incorporated.
www.churchpublishing.org

Cover design by Laurie Klein Westhafer
Typeset by PerfecType

Library of Congress Cataloging-in-Publication Data
Gordon-Young, Heather.
 Fireflies : finding light in a dark world / Heather Gordon-Young.
    pages cm
  ISBN 978-0-8192-3200-7 (pbk.) — ISBN 978-0-8192-3201-4 (ebook) 1. Gordon-Young, Heather. 2. Christian biography. I. Title.
  BR1725.G643A3 2015
  283.092—dc23
  [B]
                                    2015003958

Printed in the United States of America

1

*E*ven when we were young, the dark called to my brother in a way it didn't call to me. If such things are allotted to us somehow, if we are given ordinary measures of light and dark between us, the dark reached for my brother and not for me.

Jimmy was born complicated on the inside, in layers that I have only begun to see. The inside layers are as clear to me now as if they had always been visible: thin and delicate, translucent and veined, a glowing tissue-paper lantern, complex and iridescent as a dragonfly wing. This is where the artist lived, where the painter that he grew up to be was waiting, bathing him in the color he would bring to the canvas, the beautiful world pulsing through tiny veins, even then.

I wonder, sometimes, how long it took for the dark to notice him.

When we were little, we drove for days once to visit our cousin's farm in Ontario; my brother and I, buckled in the backseat of our new family car, watched the prairies pass by our windows like an endless golden ribbon. The farmhouse had chickens in the kitchen and cows standing at the back door.

When it got dark, Aunt Jackie took all the kids out to the field to walk in the tall grass, each of us armed with an empty pickle jar. As we walked, fireflies flew up around our ankles as if we were floating across a field of stars.

I had never seen fireflies before. I was captivated, enchanted by the night. The dark was nothing with a field of stars at your feet. If you were quick, you could catch the fireflies in your hands and put them in your jar. After a while, everyone had bright jars of fireflies but me.

"I can't catch any!" I said, embarrassed that my voice broke, as if I was crying.

"Crying's not going to make you any faster," Aunt Jackie called out from the dark.

I decided I didn't want a firefly anymore.

"Suit yourself," she said.

Later, when my aunt wasn't looking, my brother whispered to me.

"You can have mine," he said.

He loosened the lid and held the jar underneath mine to let his fireflies fill up the empty glass. That night I walked all the way back to the porch by myself, with a magic lantern of my own, as if there was no such thing as darkness.

Everybody needs a brother who can catch fireflies, I thought to myself.

I loved him fiercely.

The night our father died, I sat in the quiet of the hospice room staring at the stillness of his body. I breathed in the silence, the whispers and moaning of grieving had stopped. His wife and her daughter were there, but for a moment I had the peculiar sense of having been left, a child abandoned on a park bench in a strange town.

I had walked with him for three long months to his death, about which I could do nothing, shuffling down the dimly lit corridor to the place where he would finally leave me and go on ahead. When you lose someone you love, the world comes undone for a while.

I knew I could not go back, that night, to cups of tea and boxes of tissues at their trailer. I knew I could not offer any words of comfort to his wife, Dona. I knew I could not yet endure the tears settling into memories in the quiet of the living room, the absence of his things already packed up and put away. I knew I could not hear anyone speak his name without feeling myself smash into a thousand pieces, an icicle dropped on the cement.

"I'll come by in the morning," I said. "My things are unpacked and it's late. Probably best if we all get some sleep."

That night, when I'd left to drive to the Oasis Hotel on the highway, having left his body there under the covers, eyes closed and hands turning a bluish white, I was not more than four blocks from the hospice, when I realized I'd forgotten already the shape of his fingernails.

Already.

I wheeled the truck around and drove back fast, running to the door, ringing the midnight bell, explaining to the night nurse that I'd forgotten something. And this was true. I slipped down the nighttime hall to the empty room to study his hands one last time: the square, strong fingers, big enough to once cup both of my small hands inside them.

That night, as I lay in the hotel bed staring at the bulb on the ceiling, the mattress crinkling through the thin sheet beneath me, I dreamed of my brother, Jimmy.

It was a kind of wakeful dream.

But it must have been a dream.

He was there in the room with me, looking just the same, the same soft skin on his cheeks, but his glasses were new, or at least I didn't recognize them. He was sitting on the vinyl chair beside the bed, leaning forward, reaching out to pass me something he held in his hand.

It was a large, smooth stone, as big as a fist.

I turned onto my side and looked up at him. I didn't even say hello, I just told him straight out:

"Dad died," I said. "A few hours ago."

He said nothing; he just held the stone out for me.

I suppose he already knew.

When I sat up to reach for it, when I felt it firmly in my hand, I must have woken. He was gone and there was no stone, but my hand could still feel the weight of it, as if it had just been there.

And I knew right then what that stone had been for.

When we were little, our parents bought a cabin on Cluculz Lake from an old woman who had loved the cabin for twenty years.

"Just don't move those stones," she'd said, pointing her arthritic finger to the small circle of stones at the bottom of the hill, toward the lake. She was giving my mother a few directions before she handed over the keys.

"The flowers come up there every year, about the same time as the Blue Martens come back," she said. "The stones protect them, you'll see. Just don't move them."

I believed her. I didn't need to know then that from the beginning of time, women in quiet corners of the world had carried stones and made circles with them for protection, calling down the sacred and the divine, like some force field that would stand guard against what they feared.

Her words were authority enough. The stones would not be moved. They would circle the place the flowers belonged without wavering, without rest, through every cold winter and every long night. And every spring the green shoots pushed through the earth in the center of the circle of stones about the same week that the birds came back to live in the summer birdhouse.

When I was brave enough to explore the forest on my own, in the places where twigs snap and pine needles softly blanket the forest floor, I found a clearing, an opening in the woods, dark and gentle, circled by the trunks of strong trees. It was a place that would become mine, a place that I would carry inside myself for the rest of my life, the trees marking out a boundary, familiar and strong.

One spring, I found something in the clearing that frightened me. There were soft white feathers scattered all across the space that was mine. And when I looked further I saw a tangle of twigs up against a stump at the edge, eggshells scattered and smashed, a rounded basket-like indent in the earth, shaped by twigs and feathers, more egg shells, more feathers. And then I knew.

A terrible thing had happened.

I ran from the forest to get my father. Someone should know about this, I thought, running for help.

"Something terrible has happened!" I shouted to him.

He ran with me over the logs and through the branches and ducked inside to stand in the clearing. He stopped and scanned the ground, then looked at me with gentle eyes, relief, a look I was too young to understand. He was always good at this sort of thing.

"What do you think?" I said finally, when I'd caught my breath and been quiet long enough. "Maybe a wolf?"

He was quiet, thinking. He touched my hair with his hand and then bent down.

"Looks like a fox got in," he said, taking his hat off and reaching for a piece of white shell, studying it.

I was amazed. How calm my father seemed in the face of this. He placed the shell in my small hands and cupped them inside of his.

"But how could it?" I asked him, incredulous that this could be true. I felt my lip quiver and my eyes grow blurry with tears. "How could that happen?"

"Well, sometimes these things happen," he said.

I was certain it had been a wolf.

We were quiet.

"Do you think the mother and father were killed?"

I tried not to think of them being eaten. I tried not to notice all the feathers, scattered violently around the clearing.

He was thinking about what to say next.

"No, they're probably all right," he said. "They must have been out getting food."

I thought about what he said for a long time before I asked, because I wasn't sure I could bear the answer:

"But why did they leave their babies alone?"

"Well," he said, pausing, thinking. "Sometimes they just have to."

He could not have known then, how things would turn out.

Later that afternoon, I felt I had to do something; that there was some-thing that should be done. And so I filled my t-shirt with stones from the lake and carried them into the forest, making trip after trip until I had enough stones. I gathered the shells and feathers from the ground and put them inside the nest. Then I made a circle around the nest with the stones, marking it, protecting it. The stones would not be moved.

Many years later, when I was married with children of my own, I went back to find that place, and there, up underneath, in the same clear-ing, was the circle of stones, standing guard, marking the place that had once held a family.

The night my father died, I felt in my hand the stone that Jimmy had kept for me, for the circle of stones in the clearing.

This, I have come to realize, is why I write these pages. They are the stones I carry from the lake to tell this story: to lay the questions we could not answer on the soft ground; to mark the place on the earth that once held a family. Through every winter and every long night, the circle of stones remains for those who come to the forest long after we are gone.

2

We grew up in a tall house on Highland Drive off the Hart Highway. The town knew our neighborhood as "The Hart." The Hart was north of Prince George, straddling Highway 97 to Alaska with a handful of run-down shops that once were hopeful delicatessens or florists but had ended up trying to make a go of it as Hart Video and Hart Laundromat. By the time we grew up, the Hart had paved roads, fewer bears on the streets, and its own McDonald's.

Trees towered in our backyard. My mother used to complain that she couldn't plant a thing back there because the light from the sun never reached the ground. The backyard was a forest of thick branches and moist ground. Not even grass could find a way to grow in some places.

This is what made me bury things there, back in the darkest corner by the tire swing we never used. I buried beautiful creatures there, a soft brown bird I'd found on the side of the road, a dragonfly caught in the spokes of my bike, sometimes small treasures. Mostly the ground served as a secret graveyard.

I buried things as deeply as I could dig, which was not very deep, but you'd never notice the little graveyard unless you actually went looking. No one did. The ground was made mostly of the rot of old stumps that used to be trees long before my father built our house there, so the graveyard was covered in a thick layer of nearly black forest soil that never felt dirty to me, not even in my fingernails.

Neither the moon nor the sun could see through the trees in our backyard, at least not all the way down to the forest floor. I liked that. It was private and somehow appropriate, I felt, for burying small boxes, coffins for butterflies and mice our cat brought home. No one knew about the graves—not the sun and not even the moon. I used to think that the sun and the moon watched us, not like God, but still observing.

And perhaps it's true. Some days I still believe it, wondering what it's like to be the sun, really only ever noticing the world fully lit, always bright-edged and daylight, the right time for lemonade stands and piano lessons, for watching robins hatch from pale blue eggs in spring. This is, I think, what it means to be a child: to hold hands with the sun and look at the world together, smiling.

But the moon is different; the moon sees the world both in the day and in the night. The moon is not a stranger to darkness. The moon is silvery, cold and wise, slipping out of sight when the sun arrives. Nothing gets past the moon. Growing up has something to do with accepting the world as the moon sees it: in darkness and in light.

And when the time has come, when a child has passed from that endless sunny band of light, he slips, by force or by choice, bravely past the edge, into the place where the sunny afternoon is over and dusk begins. It is here, at the edge of darkness, where the sharp blade of night slices open the world, where the child first hears the steps of a stranger coming behind him in the dark. It is here, at the edge of night, that a child must have the courage to stand close to the moon, even if he can't bring himself to hold the moon's hand—even if the moon feels cold.

But God is different. When people come to know God, it happens, I think, in as many different ways as there are leaves on the ground after an autumn wind. I was like a child gathering dry twigs in the forest in the way that I first began to think about God, assembling them branch by branch into a fort that defined my place in amongst the tall trees, but with no roof to block the sky. It was lopsided, carefree, messy; a secret hideout, hardly distinguishable, at first, from a brush pile, unless you were the one who'd built it.

As I grew older and stronger, the branches I could carry were bigger, gathered from farther away, laid with design and attention to strength, and the fort became an elaborate structure that may not have been much to look at, but it was my own.

Still I find myself there some days, inside the meandering structure of twigs and branches. On a good day I lie flat on my back on the soft earth and peer up through the tallest trees, to the clear blue of a summer sky. Occasionally, a hummingbird or a dragonfly or some other miraculous creature dances across my view; sometimes a flock of wild geese honk their way in proper formation to the lake nearby, flying toward the voice of the one who calls them, perhaps not ever wondering whose voice it is they hear.

When I first heard this kind of voice, I was very small. Was it a voice, audible in the room, or more the feeling of a voice? I don't know. I have no idea how old I was, but I remember standing in the playroom seeing the doorknob right next to my eyes. I didn't tell anyone, of course—I seemed to know even then it might be private. I had a kind of reasoning about this strange feeling, this sense of God right there in the playroom. It wasn't logical, but I'd tried to make sense of things, the way small children do.

Perhaps, I'd reasoned, babies are born with thin, invisible ribbons attached to them, dangling them down from heaven until they find a home. And when they are safe, someone—maybe an angel—snips the ribbon. For a long time, I was certain that I was still attached somehow, that someone had forgotten. I didn't mind, of course, but my brother, I could see, was not attached, not in the same way. He seemed breakable even then.

Did I try too hard not to notice?

I was swimming front crawl in the pool to practice for my orange badge. Our family was away together on a holiday—we were at a motel. I wanted to pass the swim test when I got home, so no matter what, I kept swimming. There was someone walking along the edge of the pool trying to talk to me as I swam, an older boy with pimples, maybe a summer lifeguard. He was walking along the edge and crouching toward me, shouting at me. I think he must have been trying to correct my stroke, if I had such a thing, telling me how to move my arms, but I could only hear a word or two occasionally because my head was under the water.

I ignored him. He disappeared when I turned my face back into the water. When I lifted my head to breathe, I would notice him again. I would notice the world on the deck around him—how it went past slowly, how it all went on without me while my face was in the water, like a slow-motion movie. I liked that the boy disappeared when I turned my head. He walked away after awhile, gave up trying to talk to me.

Months later—when I am with Jimmy and nowhere near a pool—I feel exactly this feeling. It's strange and linked. I feel as if I am swimming along with my face in the pool and he is up on the ledge doing the normal things he does—cracking jokes, shouting in my face, then ignoring me. Every time I look up at him he's just the same. When I turn away from him, he disappears, like a slow-motion film.

But then, there is a moment when I lift my head out of the water to breathe and his face looks different. There is a moment when he's not looking at me or talking, but his eyes are scared, looking somewhere else. There is something sad and dark happening up there on the ledge, and when I put my face in the water it all goes on without me.

The part I do not understand is that I don't stop for this. He is crying as if something terrible has happened and for some reason I keep going under, keep going on. Am I afraid of what I see on the ledge? I like that it disappears when I turn my head. I can't stop. It's a slow-motion film that I catch only glimpses of. In one frame he is there, happy, goofing around beside me. And a few frames later something has changed, something has happened but I don't know what.

By the time I stop, by the time I lift my head from the water to call out to him, it's all over. He has wiped his tears away with the back of his hand and he tells me there's nothing the matter.

"Jimmy, what happened?" I say.

But he doesn't answer me. Not for many years.

3

*B*efore he went to prison, Mr. Diakiw taught me piano lessons for three years. I hated piano lessons. Mr. Diakiw lived a block away from our house on Highland Drive, down the hill to Montgomery Crescent, so I could easily walk to his house for lessons on Saturday morning with my John Thompson's piano book tucked under my arm.

On Saturday mornings we both pretended. I'd pretend I'd been practicing all week, holding my fingers in the shape he encouraged, and Mr. Diakiw would pretend he was interested in the lesson and that the kitchen counter was not covered with empty martini glasses. We'd both be happy when the lesson ended ten minutes early. I'd walk home as slowly as possible to make up the rest of the lesson time my parents had paid for, and no one would know the difference. Mr. Diakiw would have a long menthol cigarette in his hand ready to light the moment I stepped out the door.

One Saturday morning, when the lesson had been extra short, I walked out his driveway slowly enough to look down at my feet and notice the dusty grey colors of the small pebbles in the ditch. Not two steps away from the end of the driveway, a patch of white clover caught my eye for no reason at all. But when I bent to pick a blossom, I noticed one leaf had four smaller leaves instead of three. And when I reached for it, I noticed another on the same clump.

As I searched through the leaves, I found the whole plant was covered in four-leaf clovers. I collected them greedily, pinching the stem between my thumb and index finger, cautious but rushing, as if I might be caught, and lifted the bottom of my t-shirt to form a soft basket in which to collect them. I stripped the patch of every four-leaf clover I could find. I must have found twenty or more and carried them home in the fold of my shirt. Even my parents were amazed.

I pressed them all in separate pages of the white Bible my great-grandmother had left for me before I was born. I was already sure the book was magic with its mustard seed bauble on the zipper, and now with twenty or so four-leaf clovers tucked inside, the power in that book was certain. I took it with me to church but almost never opened it to keep the clovers safely stored inside, just in case. I knew I was a very lucky girl, with a stash of four-leaf clovers tucked in my Bible, ready to have the goodness summoned out of them whenever I needed it.

Years later I would wonder about that clover across from Mr. Diakiw's house. I would wonder if the clovers had been there for the other children— children who went to Mr. Diakiw's who could have done with a little luck, children who needed that kind of protection. I wondered if the things that went wrong had something to do with me, the luckiest girl in the world, with a secret hoard of four-leaf clovers that were meant for other people.

Mr. Diakiw was a funny man at school—a real riot in the staff room, my mother said. She was a relief teacher at our school sometimes. He was outrageous and loud, he wore vibrant colors that clashed with his wild red hair and used strange disciplinary tactics like underwear-pulls for kids who forgot their homework. Some parents complained but mostly people accepted he was just "that way," a bit different.

But he wasn't very funny on Saturday mornings at piano lessons. On Saturday mornings, I only saw Mr. Diakiw glancing at his watch and tapping the bottom of his Craven A package with a gold lighter. My piano lessons were in the study at the top of the stairs that led to the basement. The basement was the only thing that really fascinated me about piano lessons. What I really wished for was to be invited to see Mr. Diakiw's trains. Everyone knew he had a basement full of model trains with elaborate tracks, sculpted mountains, and engines that whistled when they went over bridges. From the top of the stairs, all I could see was the edge of a white table and the curve of a track. Nothing more.

"So how are your trains coming along?" I'd ask when I'd folded up my book.

Usually he ignored the question.

"I hear you've got a new bridge with real water under it," I'd say, desperate for a look.

"Yes." Long pause. "It's not ready yet though." It was clear I would not be invited down to see the trains. The trains were for Mr. Diakiw's special friends, the boys from my brother's class. But not just anyone could go; you had to be invited. There was status in being part of his inner circle.

My brother had not been invited.

But on New Year's Eve in 1975 when Jimmy was ten and in Mr. Diakiw's grade five class, my parents had a party. Mr. Diakiw was there and after several drinks my mother asked him if Jimmy could visit the trains some time.

"Of course," Mr. Diakiw said.

I wish I could have seen the look on his face.

"Well, I'm not going," Jimmy said to my mother. "I hate those kids."

"What kids?"

"The kids who go to the trains, I don't like them."

"Humph." She was annoyed. "Well you sure don't need to be complaining you've got nothing to do then. All Christmas holidays watching television! Look at the beautiful day out there; a fresh air walk down the street would be good for you." My mother was drying the dishes, pursing her lips. "You don't even know those boys. You don't see them except at school."

Funny how hard we try, as parents, to do the right things for our kids, to make them happy, to make them liked, and how wrong it all turns out sometimes.

"I see them at hockey all the time," he said. "I don't like them. I'm not going."

And this is where I stop, sometimes, when I think of him and look at my own children, who are almost grown now. I try with everything I have inside of me to know them, to know what they are frightened of, what they wish for, what lies they tell themselves. It is this intentional discovery of who these creatures are, wonderfully complicated children, that I obsess about some days, wanting to be present on the inside of their lives, as if I could enter their bloodstream and travel through their young bodies. In my mind I am striving not to shape them or fix them, but to know everything about them.

But then what? What on earth do you do with them once you've begun to see who they are, once you've noticed the layers inside, once you've been present in their bloodstream and discovered there's more than you ever imagined?

My brother was a boy with dragonfly wing layers that called for special tools, for the feathery tip of a tiny brush, perhaps angled tweezers with rubber tips. My father was a pipefitter with pipefitters' tools: a pipe wrench with jaws large enough to grab hold of a grown man's calf and never let go, a sledgehammer that could throw the weight of a dump truck behind every blow. How does a man with a pipe wrench hold this child's small fingers? How does he touch the edges of the inside layers with his heavy, greasy work gloves without leaving marks? How does a man with a sledgehammer lift this boy to the life he was born to take up?

Eventually, Jimmy went to see the trains. Not often but a few times. For the rest of the world, this occurrence was nothing.

Then he never went back.

I don't know if a shadow fell across his face the first day. I didn't know enough to stop turning my head away. I wish I could have seen him coming up the driveway afterward. I wish I'd noticed at that very moment that something had gone wrong.

That spring, my brother's class had a weeklong camping trip to Camp McGuiness. Mr. Diakiw was the boys' chaperone. Jimmy didn't want to go. He cried in his room for a week before the camp. My parents helped him pack his things in a duffle bag. He sat on the floor in the corner of his room weeping, while they put socks and underwear in the bag.

"Please don't make me go," he begged them.

"For goodness sake, Jimmy! It's only five nights. And we'll be there for family night on Wednesday." My mother had stopped being encouraging and was now just angry.

My father said nothing, just shoved his things in the duffle bag.

His son was a sissy.

At Camp McGuiness my father carried Jimmy's bag into the cabin and set it on one of the bunks. Jimmy walked behind us all. His eyes were swollen from crying. My mother told everyone she saw that Jimmy had allergies and that his eyes were red from pollen in the air. Jimmy didn't say good-bye to us. He stayed on his bunk crying when we left. Mr. Diakiw stood on the edge of the trail to wave the parents off. As we walked out of Camp McGuiness, Mr. Diakiw patted my father on the shoulder on the way by. Everything would be okay.

And this was what my parents needed: someone to tell them there was nothing wrong, that their son was fine, that they were good parents who were doing the right thing. They *needed* to believe there was nothing wrong—so they did.

This is entirely possible if you're not looking, not careful to notice what's going on inside. You will have to look deep to notice the damage. A tear on the inside seems small at first, perhaps small enough to ignore. But when the inside layer is tissue paper–thin and billowed tight, it's not strong enough to flap about in the wind without ripping wide open.

When the wind finally does come, blowing wild and strong on some ordinary afternoon, the tear opens wider, fissuring back, damaging new tissue in every gentle breeze. Maybe at first it could have been stopped, maybe at first a bit of masking tape on the edge might have helped, if we'd have seen it. But once a whole side is torn open, there's not much that a bit of tape can do.

Jimmy had been at Camp McGuiness for two nights when he found a way to call home.

"Please!" he cried into the phone. "Please let me come home. Please!" He was howling quietly on the phone, begging her. He dropped the phone without saying good-bye when my mother asked to speak to an adult.

Mr. Diakiw—who must have been standing right there—got on the phone, picking it up from dangling by the cord. "Don't worry about him—it's good for him. He needs to grow up a little. All the other boys are having a good time. He'll be fine."

When Jimmy came home from Camp McGuiness, things were different. He stopped talking to us at all, sat inside at the cabin, watched TV instead, refused to go fishing or play badminton or even swim. He cried a lot. He refused to have his photos taken. He drew pictures by himself.

"What the hell is wrong with that kid?" my father snapped, but it wasn't really a question.

I don't think he would have wanted to know the answer.

"You'd better smarten up your attitude and stop that crying, or I'll give you something to cry about," my mother said to him.

She couldn't have meant this. But she said it, the way we sometimes say things that leave marks, things we don't mean that come from our own unhappiness.

Our parents kept their unhappiness to themselves as best they could. And in so doing, my brother and I were kept away from it, on the other side of the glass, as if we lived in some kind of observation room, sealed and private from their adult lives.

We sat on the floor at the end of Jimmy's bed playing Legos, the door closed, not talking, not listening, just focusing on finding the pieces we needed. Sometimes their furious wind would blow wild and dark right through the middle of our lives, right through our house, shaking the lamps and the windows, taking down everything safe in its passing.

On those nights I tucked the white Bible under my pillow before I turned out the light. On those nights, I knew the clover was right there beneath my cheek, just in case.

4

The snow was falling softly when I made that last trip to Kelowna, up over the mountains to see my father. This time I was driving. I would be staying—until the end.

We had no idea when "the end" would come.

"Make sure you say everything you want to say now," the doctors had said. "It's always unpredictable at the end."

But what I wanted to say I couldn't form into words.

My father and I were not especially close when I was a child. I wonder if he noticed how much I admired him, how I wanted to walk like him and skip rocks the way he could.

He was not present in my life the way you might think he'd been. He worked out of town a lot, perhaps on purpose. As far as he was concerned, the boy was the father's responsibility, but the girl was the responsibility of the mother. He didn't know what to do with a daughter really, and it wasn't his concern. As a younger man I don't think he ever imagined enjoying my company someday, and I don't think he would have ever believed that there would come a day when he would need me in the way that he did.

He would look across the room at me sometimes during those last weeks and shake his head and begin to cry.

"Why are you even here?" he would stammer, and begin to weep. "Thank you for staying."

To be clear, I was not doing anything any other child would not have done, but in his rawness, I could see traces of the man he had once been, I could see him remembering his younger self: the man who had been solid and reliable and had seen his responsibilities through, but who had not really known his daughter until she was nearly a grown woman.

I think, for my father, *needing* his daughter was just so unexpected.

It was not our father who first took us to church; it was our mother. She took us to Sunday School at Knox United Church and my father stayed home. My earliest memory is not even a story, just a clip of time with sounds: just me on the stairs at the church, the cold slip of the polished railing underneath my hand on the way down to the Sunday School room, the cool musty smell of books and hymnals, the sound of the children's shiny Sunday shoes clicking on the stairs around me, echoing loudly, clicking our way down to the basement to learn stories from the Bible.

I collected those stories in my head and played them back again at night when I was falling asleep. At night the stories would blur together and become part of the same, long story, but the characters wore bright colors, and their voices sang as I passed by them on my way to sleep.

With my eyes closed I could see the disciples and the thick black waves of the ocean rolling high above the boat that Jesus and his friends were floating in. I could hear the sound of the sea gulls gathering, the nets dragging behind them, and the slosh of the water under the wooden bow.

I watched Jesus step out on the water, shouting to the waves, "Be still!" And then I could see it happen: the waves sinking, disappearing at his command, cowering under the surface of the ocean like creatures being driven to the deep.

By the time I was seven, a new church nearer to our house on Highland Drive had started meeting in the gymnasium at my school. The reverend had asked my mother to play the piano. My mother loved playing the piano on Sundays, but my father told her she wasn't allowed to play during the summer. The summers were too short as they were, and she sure wasn't going to ruin them by going to church.

When Reverend Mercer started to drop by now and again to say hello, always managing a dinner invitation, he'd stay talking to my father. And long after the dishes were done and we were off to bed, I could hear them talking at the kitchen table, my father bringing out the books he had on ancient Egypt and the Dead Sea Scrolls. Believing in God was one thing, he'd said, but he was not one to go to church; he wanted to make that clear.

But when they started to build the building—a new little church across from the ski hill—my father somehow got busy helping Reverend Mercer get it finished, even though he never wanted to get involved in the first place. And when Reverend Mercer asked my father to be on the church board while it was getting started, he agreed, even though it was the last damn thing he wanted to spend the winter doing. But this—this was how I got the key.

The first time I took the key from my father's desk, I didn't plan to use it. I just wanted to have it in my pocket when I walked by. I worried the whole way that I would lose it, keeping my hand in my pocket clasped tightly to the blue ribbon all the way through the trail, down the ski hill, and up the steep dirt road on the other side. When I got to the top, the steeple of the church was in sight. I slowed my pace, focusing on each step. I did not go into the church; I sat on the front steps and looked at the door, wondering what it was like inside when no one was there.

I put the key back in my father's desk when I got home and thought about it all week. On Tuesday after school, I slid open his desk drawer just to check that the key was still there. By Friday I had decided that using the key just once would be okay; it was not breaking the law. I would have a look inside, just for a few minutes.

So on Saturday morning I took the key from his desk early, long before I planned to walk to the church. When I set off that afternoon, I worried that people in the houses I passed would be able to tell, just by the way I walked, that I was about to do something I shouldn't. I tried to make it look as if I was on my way somewhere I was meant to be, walking purposefully.

When the key turned in the door and I felt the handle click open on the other side, there was a pounding in the back of my throat. I swallowed. I closed the door quickly behind me and stopped, leaning up against the door, catching my breath on the landing. The sound of my breathing was loud. I locked the door and started slowly up the stairs to the sanctuary.

As I climbed the stairs I could see that the church was lit with afternoon brightness, the sun reaching through the glass windows with long fingers of light.

Nothing that day was extraordinary. I sat on the front pew and watched my feet tap the carpet where the sun made patterns on the floor. I decided right then that God wouldn't mind at all if I visited again sometime.

❧

After a few weeks, I stopped slipping the key back into the drawer altogether and kept it instead in the Raggedy Ann piggy bank in my room. It was easy in the summer. The evenings were long; no one even began to wonder where I was until dark, and none of the church people bothered with church when the weather was beautiful. So for most of the summer months, except for Sundays, the empty church was mine.

In the winter it was more difficult. Night came early. I had to be careful about turning on the lights. From the outside, the church would be easily lit up like a Christmas tree; anyone driving by would spot the lights on. I would use only the light on the piano to soften the dark of the sanctuary, bending its gooseneck down close to the wood to diffuse the brightness. When it was cold it took time to get the heat started.

And the snow was problematic. If there had been fresh snow, my tracks would be obvious. Sometimes I would shuffle my feet around the parking lot in the dark to mimic a dog running, though the next day it never quite looked like I'd imagined.

I would center the hymnals in the pew racks or straighten the church library. Sometimes I would polish the wide wooden altar at the front carved with the words: "Do this in remembrance of me." My fingers traced the letters, memorizing the way they felt under my fingertips.

Even though the winter was more difficult, it was also my favorite time to be there. It was mysterious, magic. Sometimes it was so cold I could see my breath, and it looked to me as if my soul were swirling out into the church when I breathed out deeply.

I sat by the heaters at the front near the cross—not for any religious reason, but because it was warmest there and a huge velvet curtain hung to the floor behind the cross. When the church was cold enough, the wood in the walls made cracking noises in the freezing temperatures. I would pull the velvet curtain up over my shoulders and let the heat fill the curtain around me like a hot air balloon.

This was when I first began to notice God. It wasn't that God had just arrived—I knew that. It was gentler than that, as if I'd become still enough to notice there was someone else in the room. This sudden feeling of someone's eyes on me, almost as if they had touched my skin, took my breath.

Once at our cabin on Cluculz Lake, when the relatives were visiting and the sun was almost down, I wandered off to the boathouse and got my casting rod out. I switched lures from my favorite Mepps Black Fury to a plain silver spinner to try to catch the last of the evening light out on the water. My first cast was terrible; the lure dropped into the water near a snag.

But my second cast that day was something else—almost miraculous.

I leaned back and threw my whole shoulder forward, releasing the orange button at exactly the right moment; the lure flew through the sky pulling the line with it tight and strong with just the right curve. It flew so far I thought it had disappeared. Then with a deep throaty noise that I could feel travel all the way to my hands, the lure hit the water gracefully and sunk, way out where the sun still shimmered. I let it sink for a second and then began the slow reel in, feeling the tension of the lure pull against the line just as it should. It was perfect, fish or no fish.

And at that moment I felt it: someone watching me, as if I could feel something on my shoulder.

I glanced around quickly to the shore and there he was, settled into a rickety lawn chair, up against the old boathouse where no one would notice him; there was Grandpa Young. He was quiet, watching the water. His hands were perched on the plastic handles, a cigarette resting in the corner of his mouth. Grandpa Young never seemed to get smoke in his eyes. When I noticed him, I felt my face flush.

He didn't say a word. He just nodded a little and stared straight at me, not quite smiling. Then he looked out to the water again, his chin raised slightly, scanning the glassy surface and I knew exactly what he meant by that. I knew he meant for me to try again, that he expected I could do better; that I'd done good but he knew there was more in me yet. And from then on, even when I was alone on the dock, even after he'd died, I could feel him there, always.

And this was how it began to feel in the church that winter, when I was especially still with the velvet curtain tucked up to my chin. I hadn't noticed God there at first, but afterward, once I'd seen him sitting across the sanctuary with his arm up on the bench, a cigarette resting in the corner of his mouth, never once getting smoke in his eyes, I could feel him there, always.

5

By the time I was eleven, I was much older than the other children in the Sunday School room. Mrs. Meldrum was away and Mrs. Graham was helping out teaching the story of Noah's Ark. I felt strangely large when Mrs. Graham looked at me, not cute and wide-eyed like the wee children gathered on the mat at the front. I was enormous, my knees pointed up too high as I perched on the edge of a tiny chair built for five-year-olds.

I had seen the same felt board Ark be placed on the blue background every year, the same white-bearded Noah, the same family members crouching by the table in the Ark. I remembered the same tattered cardboard edges, the pairs of dogs and cows and sheep and monkeys and lions and wolves.

When I asked Mrs. Graham if I could put up the giraffes, she said, without thinking, "No." When I raised my hand to ask to put on the monkeys, she asked me to leave the board to the younger children.

"Could I at least put on the waves at the end?" I said, preparing to settle.

"No, not today, stop asking. Period."

When all of the characters were inside the Ark and someone put on the raindrops, we knew the story was coming to a finish.

I hadn't planned to ruin the lesson that day but I had a question. I knew it would annoy Mrs. Graham if I raised my hand to ask her, but it seemed like a fair question. I raised my hand.

She ignored me for a while and then looked at her watch. "Is it a quick question? We're nearly out of time," she said.

"Yes," I said. "I was wondering why there are no felt board pictures for the dead people."

She blinked a few times and didn't answer.

"What I mean is, shouldn't we have some of their bodies floating by in the water? Maybe we should make new characters to put up for the drowning people."

She blinked again.

"No" was all she said.

I thought for a while. She stared at me.

"Why not?" I asked her. By then I genuinely wanted to know.

I expected her to say that it was inappropriate to put up dead bodies on the felt board, or that they had floated away, or that she would ask the Reverend Mercer about it. Instead she said something quite different.

"We don't have felt board characters for them," she said. "They're not part of the story. The story is about the good people and the animals who were inside the Ark. It's not about the bad people who were drowned in the flood."

❧

I had not expected her to say that the dead people were not part of the story.

I had not expected her to say that the children and the grandmothers and the babies who drowned in the flood did not matter.

That night I went to bed and thought for a long time. I could see them all in my mind, swimming toward the big boat, holding on to floating logs, banging on the doors of the big wooden Ark.

"Help us! Let us in!"

There was a girl screaming out for her mother who was facedown in the water, not answering; just white, dead, floating. The girl's arms were wrapped tightly around a floating log, she had gashes on her shoulder and a cut on her face.

"Mommy!" she screamed. The girl, I realized, was one of the bad people who would soon be dead. I wondered what she'd done.

Inside the boat I could see Noah and his family, sitting quietly around the table, chewing mouthfuls from their bowls of rice, staring down at the floor, saying nothing, just chewing, trying to block out the sounds of the people dying outside, trying to ignore the pounding on the doors of the boat.

"Can't we open the doors just a little?" Noah's son said.

Noah shook his head.

"Rules are rules, son," he said. "Rules are rules."

When I was a child, I loved a dog that was not my dog, but I pretended he was. His name was King. I loved him more than my own dog, but I didn't let on. He was an old German Shepherd, a retired police dog who lived on Montgomery Crescent with Mr. Dickson. He roamed the neighborhood with the kids who played in the front yards. When I first met King, his back was nearly as high as my armpit. He was silent, never barked or growled. He was usually dusty from lying in the dirt at the edge of our games. When he heard Mr. Dickson whistle for him to come home, he turned and ran. No matter what.

I didn't know there were dogs that would obey like that.

Once, a young Lab in heat escaped from her yard. When King mounted her, I didn't know what he was doing.

"They're humping, you idiot!" someone said.

When it was over, they were stuck together, joined at the genitals and we all giggled. Then King heard a whistle. He struggled and whined and yelped, pulling free and ran for home. It was the strangest thing I'd ever seen. It was the first time I'd heard King make a noise.

Then one day, another very strange thing happened. It was late summer and we were playing Frozen Tag on our lawn. There was a terrible barking coming from up the hill where King was chained when his owners were away. We all looked up from the game and in seconds there was King, bolting down the hill, right past us, his chain dragging on the ground behind him. We could hear Mr. Dickson shouting and whistling for him, but King didn't stop.

And then we saw it.

In the middle of the road, not fifty meters away from us, a huge black bear was coming down the street in a slow stagger, its head swinging back and forth. And when King barreled into his side, the bear and the dog tumbled across the gravel like a ball of flying dirt. The two black bodies disappeared, tumbling into the bush, snarling, yelping, biting, like I'd seen in a cartoon. It happened so fast, no one had time to be frightened. Mr. Dickson came running down the street with his baseball cap in his hand shouting and swearing, but the dog didn't come.

A few hours later, King reappeared hobbling down the street, heading for home. He had gashes in his left side and a torn ear, the length of his chain was still dragging behind him. Mr. Dickson said he didn't know what the hell had happened. He'd gotten out of the car, he said, they'd just pulled in the driveway and King was already running to the end of the chain. The chain snapped and King flew down the hill. He figured the bear up the road was a coincidence, maybe. He just didn't know what got into that dog.

We heard him tell some adults in our driveway that the dog was *ruined*, that he should probably send him off to the farm. He didn't let King off his chain anymore. We brought him scraps from our dinners for a few days while it still felt like an adventure. Then mostly everyone forgot.

But I couldn't forget. I thought about it every night. I guessed that King was *ruined* because he didn't follow Mr. Dickson's rules.

Following the rules, I guessed, was somehow more important than doing the right thing.

6

When our father built our house on Highland Drive, he tried to leave as many trees as he could. He altered the plans for the front of the house so it made room for the old pine tree that had been there long before we came along, when the lot was still a forest. There was a young birch, just a few feet tall, growing next to the house, when he strapped the deck on the front. The deck would now reach out over the little tree, creating a ceiling that must have startled the small tree, blocking out the light. Rather than take the tree down, they decided to wait, to see what happened.

That tree survived by suddenly growing sideways, by forcing a ninety degree bend in its trunk so that it grew horizontally for awhile and then sprung up to clear the edge of the deck, breaking all the rules about the way trees are meant to grow, finding the light by its own modification. The bend in the tree would be present always, even when the trunk was as a thick as my father's leg. Years later, I'm sure that tree remembered. I'm sure it knew that it was forever altered by what happened all those years ago.

I was six years old when I met Ella. She came to our kindergarten class at Austin Road Elementary on a sunny autumn day in 1974. The school

27

system was trembling under the weight of change and so was Ella. But none of us kids knew it. We didn't guess that the schools were experimenting with integration, deciding whether or not kids like Ella could belong with the rest of us.

Ella had sparkling brown eyes and thick dark eyebrows that moved on her face like caterpillars when she watched us. She was much bigger than the rest of us, taller and big boned, but she seemed younger, somehow.

Mrs. Ellicott had taken me aside privately that morning; her face was serious.

"Heather," she said, staring right in my eyes, "We have a new girl coming to school today," she'd said. "I was hoping you'd be her friend when she arrives."

"Sure," I said. "I don't mind." I could see there was more to it, but she wasn't letting me in on it.

Ella did not sit on the small kindergarten chair beside her mother. Instead she sat half on her lap, her face buried in her mother's blouse. Mrs. Fenton whispering in her ear, soothing, coaxing, wishing.

And because I could see how much it mattered to Mrs. Fenton, I wanted to be brave. When I said hello to Ella, she did not say hello back. I invited her to sit on the carpet with me but she turned her face away and lifted her wrist to her mouth, pressing her skin into her teeth, biting her arm softly.

"She's a bit shy," Mrs. Fenton said. "Maybe a little later."

Mrs. Fenton had the same dark eyebrows and the same square forehead.

"That's okay," I said to her. "I used to be shy too."

But to everyone's surprise, Ella followed me back to the carpet and nearly sat on top of me.

When the whole class started to giggle, Ella lifted her arm to her mouth and bit her wrist hard, screeching.

Everyone stopped laughing, worried.

I glanced over at her mother who seemed not to notice at all. In fact, Mrs. Fenton's cheeks were glowing, smiling; Ella stopped screeching and pressed close beside me on the carpet.

Later that week, when Mrs. Fenton was not in the room, something upset Ella and because I was next to her, she grabbed my arm, shoved it in her mouth and bit down hard with her teeth. There were red marks on my arm when I got home.

The principal called my parents that night to explain.

At dinner that night my father was annoyed.

"I'd like to know what kind of world this is when *my* child has to look after somebody else's retarded kid at school?"

Shamefully, people still used that word then.

"That kid shouldn't even be at school. It's ridiculous!"

I was ashamed of him for saying this. Perhaps, I thought to myself, six-year-olds were better at understanding kids like Ella. I kept nearly everything about her a secret after that.

When she bit me I didn't tell them.

The marks on my wrist were private.

Sometime during the next school year, Mrs. Fenton and her daughter rented a house a few blocks down the street from ours. As far as I could tell, Ella didn't have a father, but in those days it was rude to ask, and I knew it.

My mother began to recognize Mrs. Fenton in the grocery store or driving by. My mother and Mrs. Fenton were pleasant to each other but I didn't see Ella much. She'd been put in a "special class." After school one day, Ella came to play at our house. My brother and I pushed her up and down our driveway in his go-cart. She bit her wrist the whole time and laughed. We took turns riding on the back of the go-cart.

"Fast!" she yelled. "Fast!"

After awhile, my brother stopped the go-cart at the end of the driveway, putting his foot under the back wheel to stop it from rolling. He stared across the street, thinking.

"What?" I said. "What are you doing?"

He didn't answer my question.

"Come on," he said. "Push."

We snuck the go-cart down the street and pushed it all the way to the top of the steep hill on Montgomery Crescent.

"Are you scared?" I asked Ella.

"Fast!" she yelled, jumping up and down, climbing in. We checked for cars behind us, then Jimmy and I stepped on to the back and held on for dear life. We screamed till our throats were raw as the go-cart flew down the hill, the wheels shaking, the boards creaking, the world blurring, Ella clapping, me praying, dear God don't let the wheels fall off.

They didn't. We would remember that day forever.

On Ella's birthday that year, Mrs. Fenton called to ask if I could come to her birthday party. My mother said, of course I could. We ate cake and played with a hula-hoop in the backyard for what seemed like a very long time. There was just Mrs. Fenton, Ella, and me.

"Is it time for me to go home yet?" I asked Mrs. Fenton, trying to hold a smile in my voice.

"Not quite yet," she called out from her lawn chair.

I would go to Ella's birthday party every year for four years, and every year there would be just the three of us and a cake. Mrs. Fenton smiled the whole time and Ella laughed, sometimes biting her wrist when we played.

By the time we were ten, I almost never saw Ella. She was often away from school. She was sick, they said. And when Mrs. Fenton called that year to ask if I could come to Ella's birthday party—I lied.

"I'm sorry," I said to her. "I can't—I've got a Brownie bottle drive that afternoon."

It was the first thing I thought of.

I didn't tell my mother or anyone else about the phone call.

The next week my mother and I saw Mrs. Fenton in the grocery store and when she asked about the Brownie bottle drive, my mother told her I didn't go to Brownies anymore, that I'd given it up the year before, which was a shame, she'd said.

Mrs. Fenton looked, at that moment, utterly lost, as if she might suddenly break into pieces on the floor right there beside the onions and the potatoes.

I looked away.

Mrs. Fenton never called again.

Ella never came back to our school.

By the time I was twelve, I was nearly finished with figure skating lessons. Not because I was an excellent skater, but perhaps because I was not. The theme of the Spring Figure Skating Carnival was *April Showers, April Flowers*, which meant all fifty some skaters were dressed as blossoms: Blue Bells, Daffodils, Tiger Lilies, Daisies, Tulips, Sunflowers.

Even the head coach, Patty, dressed up as the gardener in a peppy little number that was both low cut and cute as a button. Patty was a dynamite skater but nasty if you crossed her. People used to whisper about her behind her back.

I was not a graceful skater, but I was a good leader.

I paid attention, knew the cues, and followed the rules.

I was thoroughly reliable.

I was made *Head Daffodil* because of it.

Patty could count on me.

The Carnival dress rehearsal and performance night were the only time we got to see the whole skating school all together. From a distance I could see that all the flower costumes improved once we were together out on the ice, much more like a garden. With the lights up and the music filling the arena, the odd stitching and glued-on sequins didn't seem to matter.

At the dress rehearsal, the Daffodils and Blue Bells shared the dressing room next to the coach's office. Just before we were cued to line up, I heard shouting, two voices I knew well, but only Coach Patty's I could place.

"I don't care how much money you paid, she's only been to three practices all year!"

It was Patty.

The other voice was harder to hear, angry whispering, someone trying to be civilized.

Then Patty again: "Don't you think for one minute that your daughter is going to wreck my show, lady!"

Then the lady let her have it: "You listen to me, you smart-ass bitch. This is not *your* show or your private exhibition! This is the *children's* performance, not yours! My daughter will be taking part in the Carnival tomorrow whether you like it or not. She will not be here today because she's sick, but she will be here early tomorrow. And I will sue you so fast your head will spin if you refuse her and you *know* I can do it. I will see you tomorrow!"

It was Mrs. Fenton.

Mrs. Fenton arrived at the Carnival holding Ella by the hand. Ella looked nearly the same as she did when she first came to kindergarten, just taller, bigger. She was twelve, now, like me. She had the world's biggest sunflower strapped to the top of her head and a bright yellow dress. Mrs. Fenton did not take Ella into the Sunflowers' dressing room. Instead she sat with her on the bench outside, holding her hand, and together they watched all the skaters going by in their flower costumes.

I wondered if I should go and say hello, but I didn't.

The rules were clear: we were all to stay in our dressing rooms until we were called.

The rules were a relief. I didn't know what to say.

I heard Coach Patty telling the Sunflowers to just go on with their performance no matter what, that Ella would be there but not to let that be a distraction. Ella would *not* ruin their routine if they just ignored her and went on.

Coach Patty obviously didn't want to be sued.

The whole evening had gone well, each flower group had dazzled the crowd with their routines—spins and loops on the ice, circles and turns—then scurried back into the changing rooms until the Grand Finale. I was part of the older group of skaters; we sat quietly in the bleachers after our turn.

Ella was a Sunflower. Most of the girls in her group were seven years old and only half as tall as Ella. She towered above them in true Sunflower style. Mrs. Fenton left Ella standing with the other Sunflowers by the ice and found a seat on the bleachers nearby.

When it was their turn, they skated onto the ice but Ella did not go with them. Instead she stayed behind the boards watching them all go round and round, her head bumping softly, rhythmically against the glass.

Mrs. Fenton sat in the bleachers craning her neck from the aisle, but Ella did not skate onto the ice.

The coach rolled her eyes at a parent who was sitting behind me. I heard the parent say, "Just look at that kid—it's ridiculous to even have her here."

The Grand Finale was set to *Raindrops Keep Falling on My Head*. It would be the highlight of the evening. All the skaters on the ice, each bouquet of flowers in spinning circles, the older girls in position to form a can-can lineup that would span the rink. Coach Patty in her bouncy gardener outfit was preparing to weave in and out of the flowers, scattering sparkles that were meant to look like raindrops.

As Head Daffodil, I knew the cue to wait for. I knew exactly what to do. We stood in formation, toes picked into the ice and hands positioned gracefully. The Blue Bells finished their circle and the Sunflowers began to step onto the ice.

And there, right behind the gathering of little Sunflowers, stepping awkwardly onto the ice, was Ella, the biggest Sunflower of them all.

The Sunflowers were quick to glide to center ice, but Ella was not. Ella's ankles were shaking, nearly giving out beneath her.

She turned to look back for the safety of the doors she'd just come through, but her skates slipped out from underneath her.

One girl looked back to see if she was okay, but the Head Sunflower shouted, "Come on—we're supposed to leave her!"

The Sunflowers skated on.

At that moment I felt God right there in the arena. I couldn't see him, but I knew he was there somewhere in the bleachers, a cigarette in the corner of his mouth, looking out at me. I knew he was looking over at Ella, his chin lifted a little, waiting for me to do the right thing.

"You go on without me," I said to the Daffodils behind me.

"What are you *doing*?" they snapped, but I ignored them.

"Just go without me!"

I skated over to Ella and stopped just beside her so I wouldn't frighten her.

"Ella?" I said to her in a friendly whisper. "It's me, Heather."

I hoped she remembered me. I held out my hand.

She looked up at me with her bright brown eyes, her caterpillar eyebrows wriggling. It took her a moment or two and then she smiled and squealed. She reached for my hand and I helped her up.

When we were both steady, we linked our arms and laughed. Ella shoved her free arm in her mouth and bit her wrist hard.

I thought of the go-cart flying down Montgomery Crescent.

"C'mon" I said. "Let's skate fast!"

I heard the music filling the air around us, I heard the man singing about raindrops, singing about being free, and I realized I was freer than I'd ever been in my whole life.

There was a freedom in me that I cannot explain.

It was the freedom that birds must feel when they first fly. It was the freedom of doing the right thing. It was the freedom of breaking the rules.

The audience was on their feet, whistling and cheering, and to this day I don't know if it was because Patty had just pulled off a toe loop jump or because they were happy to see Ella skating, but it didn't matter for a second. Ella and I skated around and around the rink, and through the bright lights I could see Mrs. Fenton, jumping up and down, clapping and shouting out, blowing her girl kisses.

7

$\mathcal{M}$y brother's silence had been noticeable for some time, but it grew and grew, filling up the space between us, as if the glass that separated even us was now three feet thick and opaque. Through the glass I could catch glimpses of my family, blurred figures moving silently on the other side.

No one knew why my brother sat alone in the cabin on sunny days, why he refused to go swimming, why he cried when my parents got angry, and why he could not stop. None of us knew that things had begun to go terribly wrong, that the tissue paper layer inside of him had begun to tear in the wind.

No one knew, then, why he began to draw obsessively, filling sketchbooks with animals and birds at first. But as Jimmy grew older and the silence grew thicker, enormous beasts with violent jaws would appear on the pages, dark creatures reaching from the center of the earth, then the bony claws of skeletons reaching up from some gravesite clawing at the flesh of a figure, a young man whose scream could not be heard from the page.

"Teenagers!" my mother would say. "You sure like that gory stuff. Why don't draw nice animals again?"

He never answered her; he just went back downstairs and closed the door. By the time my brother was fifteen, we no longer belonged to each other; it was as if I hardly knew him at all.

For as long as we had been on Highland Drive, our family had watched a pair of robins arrive in the tree beside our deck every year. I didn't know it then, but the spring that my brother was fifteen would be the last spring we'd watch the robins.

The robins would begin the repairing of the nest each year, fluffing with new bits of softness they gathered from around the yard to make the nest cozy for the eggs, as if the nest was a cottage that had been shut up for winter. And every year, my brother and I had waited for the delicate blue eggs to appear, leaning over the railing to peer down into the nest.

It had become a family ritual, an assurance that all was well with the world, the winter over and yes, here was spring, just as we expected. Each year we welcomed the same birds back to the nest, greeting them as if they were friends we hadn't seen in months. It didn't matter whether or not it was true—whether or not they really were the same birds—what mattered was that we believed them to be the same, year after year, ushering in the bright hope of summer.

The birds always arrived within a day or two of Mother's Day. But the spring that Jimmy was fifteen, the birds were already three weeks late when I began to take action. On Saturday I drew huge, thick arrows in pink chalk on our driveway, big enough to be visible from the sky and pointing toward the nest. I wrote *ROBINS THIS WAY*.

"That's stupid," my brother said. "Robins can't read signs."

"How do *you* know?" I spat back at him. "Maybe they can." Of course they couldn't. I knew that. But the next day, the robins actually did arrive, and although I never confessed it to my brother, I was genuinely surprised.

In time, the eggs hatched and the tiny peeping had grown into noisy squawking. There were five babies in the nest that year—every other year there'd been four.

"Must be a lucky year," our mother said.

Then one night a terrible storm came through, thundering and blowing hail and rain, taking trees down all along Highland Drive as if an angry giant had come through with a machete. The neighbor's window was smashed from branches broken off in the night. The next morning, though it was still secure in the crook of the birch tree, the nest was empty. And even though the sun was shining, as if it didn't know the night before had happened, the morning was silent, as if every bird that ever was had disappeared in the storm.

"Maybe they flew away," my mother said while we scanned the nest and the ground from our deck. "Stranger things have happened."

No one believed her.

Instead, we began searching the ground, lifting bushes and listening, freezing in our tracks at the first sound of anything bird-like. We found three of the baby birds in a huddle, up under a decorative shrub, shivering and scared. The other two, we agreed, had probably not made it.

In the hope that the mother would return to the nest, my father climbed a ladder and placed the babies back in the tree with gloved hands that cupped their small bodies. He opened a new package of thick canvas gloves so he wouldn't get the smell of humans on their feathers.

"Never touch a wild animal with your hands," he reminded us. "It's a very selfish thing to do to an animal. The mother will abandon them."

And even though it was a lesson I had heard all my life, it was not a lesson that I had really taken to heart. The desire to reach out and touch the small peeping birds was unshakable. Instead, my father let us climb the ladder and feed the babies worms. They opened their beaks wide and stretched their throats open to the sky so that I could dangle the worm above their beaks and see all the way into their stomachs.

The next day, as we'd all hoped, the mother robin returned to the nest. And, because it was Sunday and there was not much else to do, I decided to search for the missing two birds. I didn't believe they could have flown away or simply disappeared in the wind. If nothing else I knew their bodies would be somewhere and if I could find them, I'd bury them properly in the backyard.

As I searched the back of the neighbor's garden near the vegetable patch, I heard a tiny peep. Up in behind a fallen sawhorse, trembling and hungry, was the missing pair. When I pulled the sawhorse back, they squawked like they were angry. At that moment, I forgot the lesson my father had tried to teach us, I forgot about everything but the fact that I had found them.

I reached for the two small creatures with both hands, intending to tuck them into the cradle I would make with my soft cotton shirt and run to show my brother. But as I felt the heat of their soft animal bodies for the first time, the life of the small birds wiggling in my hands, it was as if I held the universe in my fingers, as if the sun and the moon at once wiggled in the palms of my hands and I dared not squeeze them or drop them, but could not let them go.

Never before had I felt this strange feeling, the wiggling warmth of a small wild body, a forbidden pleasure, grasped in my tiny fingers. And when I woke from this moment, jarred by the squawking of the mother robin on the fence nearby, I knew I had done a very foolish thing.

Of course, I hadn't meant to keep the small creatures. Truly I had not, at first. But once I had them in a shoebox in my closet, it seemed like the only sensible thing to do. I had, after all, sentenced them to a motherless life the moment I'd grabbed them. I could only see two options: to leave them to die on their own on the ground or to look after them. It would be my penance for such stupidity: digging worms everyday, changing the tissues that lined the box, teaching them to fly on the front lawn.

I didn't really believe that my family wouldn't discover the birds, but I'd hoped to have the birds healthy in my care before they found out; I knew I'd be misunderstood. They'd think I'd taken the birds on purpose, hidden them selfishly away. They wouldn't understand I'd had no choice, that I'd already ruined the birds when I'd touched them.

What I had not expected was my brother's anger. I had not expected him to feel wounded himself by the birds in the box. It was as if he could not stand to be near them, couldn't bear the pain he felt as he thought of them captured, trembling in the box. And he couldn't stand to be near me, knowing what I'd done. He could not, I could see, bear to stand there and watch them slowly die.

"They'll have to go outside," my father said. "The healthy one needs to go back in the nest. The other one doesn't look like it's going to make it."

"I can look after them!" I protested. "I know what to do—I have worms for them!"

My brother swore at me under his breath and went downstairs.

"I thought you said the mother would abandon them?" I asked my father.

"Who knows? Maybe she won't," he said. "It's worth a try. We'll put the strong one up in the nest. I'll take care of the sick one."

I knew what he meant.

"Dad!" I begged him. "Let me look after it; maybe it *will* get better, you don't know for sure!" He shook his head, as if he knew better but couldn't face the argument.

Outside all the other birds had faired well and had begun to flit from branch to branch. Even the one we placed last in the nest leapt up within a day or two; the mother hadn't seemed to notice the bird had been touched.

But the bird in the box was not well. At first it had looked like it might be getting stronger. We put the box in the basement near the furnace where it was warm. It ate a few worms the first day, but after that it stopped eating at all and lay very still.

"Oh well," my mother said as we watched the small bird by the furnace get sicker and sicker. "Five is a big number for one season anyway. That mother had four that made it! That's a good year for sure."

My mother had pronounced the bird's death, but I would continue to hope.

The day I tried to force its beak open, my brother stood behind me watching.

"Don't you get it? He'll *never* get better! He's all damaged inside. Why don't you get that?"

"How do *you* know?" I demanded. "He could get better tomorrow, we don't know."

"All you're doing is making him suffer! He's never *ever* going to get better!" my brother said, tears filling his eyes. "Why can't you fucking see that? You're so selfish!"

He walked away and slammed his bedroom door.

On Wednesday night my parents were both out. I went down to check on the robin. This time his mouth was wide open, so for a minute I thought he was hungry. I reached for a worm, but then I saw his chest moving: heaving in and out, gasping for air.

He was not hungry.

He couldn't breathe.

When I reached into the box and picked him up, a smelly brown liquid ran down my wrist. That was when I knew he would die.

The last thing I wanted to do was to get my brother; but it was the only thing I could think of.

Jimmy came running and looked into the box.

When he saw the bird gasping for air, he let out a sob.

"Oh my God!"

I didn't say a word.

Jimmy made a fist that went white and punched the wall.

He bent down and reached into the box.

"Come here little guy," he said in a small voice. "I'm sorry little fella."

He was crying. He lifted the bird out of the box and carried him to the back door, shaking. He kicked the screen door open with his foot and went to the woodpile. He grabbed the axe from the wall.

Jimmy put the bird down gently on a stump. His hands were shaking. He held the axe in both hands and stared down at the bird. He was crying so hard, his chest was heaving in and out; he was trying to breathe by sucking air through his teeth. He lifted the axe high above his head and cried out with a terrible sob as he drove the axe three inches into the wood, severing the bird's head in an instant. He didn't move. He stood by the stump, his hands gripping the handle of the axe and his head hanging down to his chest.

I was crying too, but I hadn't noticed. I sat on the woodpile and stared at the blood on the chopping block for a long time, my heart no longer pounding but shivering. Silent tears leaked from my eyes.

I went inside to get a small box. I put clean tissues in it and picked up the bird's body and then his head. I wrapped him softly and made a nest with the tissues. Then I drew a cross on the box and got a shovel. I buried the box in the backyard and I prayed for the little bird. I tried to think of him flying in heaven but I couldn't.

All I could see was the bird on the chopping block: his chest heaving in and out, gasping for air.

And when I closed my eyes, all I could see was my brother, his knuckles white on the handle of the axe, tears running down his face, his chest heaving in and out, gasping for air.

8

The summer I was thirteen, I stopped things. I stopped wearing the homemade polyester slacks my mother sewed; I stopped taking figure skating lessons and writing poetry; and I stopped walking to the church in the evenings by myself.

Instead, I walked the neighborhood after dark with the new friends I'd made that year in high school. They let me borrow their eyeliner in the bathroom when I got to school. I was nearly blind without my glasses, so I would get up on the bathroom counter on my knees to get close enough to see in the mirror. It did not occur to me, in those days, to ask myself what on earth I was doing.

When I look at photos, I can see I was the smart kid they were saving. They taught me to inhale when I smoked, but eventually, because I was the overachiever, I taught them to blow smoke rings and discovered the power of a few party tricks to ease any remaining social barriers.

But the summer I was thirteen, my brother turned sixteen. Jimmy's party tricks were different. My father offered him his "first beer" on his sixteenth birthday. It was August. My brother grabbed it full fisted, tipped his head back, and downed it. The beer disappeared down his throat.

At first no one said anything. But then my father gave his shoulder a shake in a take-it-easy-young-fella kind of way, surprised at his son's proficient handling of a beer. But a little twinkle of something else was in his eye. Was it pride? Perhaps his son was not a sissy after all.

By the next summer, we knew our parents' marriage was crumbling. It was not the first year that we noticed our mother was unhappy, but it was the first year that nothing else seemed to matter—to anyone. It was the first summer we stopped going to the cabin as a family, the first summer they left us at home alone for weekends, the first year I could see great chunks of our lives falling to pieces. It was the first year I knew, without a doubt, that something terrible was beginning to happen to my brother, but there was no one to notice but me.

I believe he found himself freezing on the inside, the cold drip-dripping of fear that had echoed inside his chest as a boy, the damp cave he lived inside of was now not only wet, but icy cold; cold in the way ice burns, the way ice can sever a limb with its teeth.

So he'd started a fire inside himself, the way people who are lost sometimes do, a small one at first, mostly twigs and grasses, little shavings of anger, to take the edge off the cold, to stop the freeze. He would warm himself next to it, sipping from a bottle of vodka he stashed under the couch, holding his palms up to the flame, an angry, distant heat that kept back the ice, angry at the world. He was careful at first, keeping the flames small, shuffling the wood gently to keep the coals hot without flame. He drank secretly, lived secretly. But in those days, I suppose, living secretly was what we both did.

It was Sunday morning. My parents were away for the weekend.

"What are you *doing*?" I said, startled to see him there, genuinely puzzled, when I caught him crouching down at the bottom of our parents' liquor cabinet at 8 a.m. I was coming in from the front deck with Dad's ashtray in one hand, my cigarettes in the other.

"What are *you* doing?" he spat back at me, glaring at the cigarettes. He took out a large glass, poured the clear liquid from the bottle, leaving a bit of room for orange juice. I watched, incredulous. Afterward he refilled the bottle with water and held it up to check he'd gotten the level right. That was the first time I knew.

He'd just turned seventeen.

After this exchange, he was no longer careful around me. He drank, I smoked. We didn't discuss it.

When my parents went away, Jimmy was careless with the fire, he sat alone beside it, drinking heavily, stoking the flames, stacking it high with whatever he could find, the flames reaching up, scorching the inside of the cave and melting the ice in great sheets of water that rushed into currents swirling around his ankles, tugging at him, pulling him under. From my room I could hear the water sloshing in the cave, pouring down, nearly drowning him.

I was afraid. I covered my ears to keep out the sounds. I was never more alone than when it began to get dark, when I knew the whole night was ahead of us, that I would wait alone, a pillow on my head, staring at the light in the hall that illuminated my room, measuring the width of the band of light it let in every time I opened my eyes. I would know if someone had moved my door.

And sometimes, when I couldn't stand it any longer and didn't know what else to do, I would go to find him, sitting on the couch alone, the fire raging inside of him, the melt water spilling out from his eyes, his shoulders shaking, hungry for someone to sit with him while the flames burned.

"You okay?" I'd say, knowing the answer.

"You want a drink?" he'd say.

"No, I'm good."

And we'd sit there until I was sure he wouldn't drown.

Sometimes, in the middle of the night, when my parents were away, I would wake up with a strange terror already awake inside of me, beating its wings against my chest, before I was even conscious. My room felt peculiar, the air disturbed, as if someone had been there watching me.

There was no one.

But sometimes, I would open my eyes and see him there—my brother, just standing, his silhouette leaning up against my doorframe, the hall light bright behind him, the house silent. Even with the hall light on, the room felt darker than the night itself.

"What are you doing?" I'd say.

"Shhh . . . nothing," he'd say, watching me.

"Jim, what are you doing? Go to bed! It's the middle of the night."

I would say this fiercely, not letting him see the terror inside of me. I would sit up straight, making myself bigger and more forceful.

"Okay, sorry, sorry, sorry," he'd say, his voice thick with alcohol. As if he'd just come to his senses. He would go then, scolded.

But sometimes the dark was charged with something sinister, something beyond our control; I could feel it. I worried he would lose his mind and do something he didn't mean to do, but I didn't know what.

Once, I got up and found him wrapped in a blanket on the floor in the hallway outside my door, his glasses twisted sideways on his head as he slept, the smell of sleep and alcohol and breathing, the smell of my brother. I didn't wake him. I shut my door and pushed a chair up against it. I went back to bed, thinking about my parents.

In the morning he was gone and the blanket was folded up and put away. I never mentioned it. Whole years of our lives were swallowed by this darkness; it was a darkness I couldn't talk about. Not to anyone.

I thought of the feathers scattered in the clearing of the forest. I wanted to run to my father shouting, "Something terrible is happening to us!" But neither my father nor my mother had any strength to come to the edge of the forest; neither of them could hear us calling out from that dark place.

I would spend my teenage years carrying stones into the forest every weekend, building a circle to protect us. Just don't move those stones, I said out loud some nights, when the darkness crept in thick and cold. It was the only thing I knew how to do. And even though my brother and I were together, the circle of stones I'd laid around us was not high enough to keep out the wolf.

9

Nobody wakes up one day and thinks, "Today I think I'll ruin my life." Nobody plans on becoming an alcoholic. Addiction is a silent being that stalks you from the day you're born, long before you ever take that first drink. Addiction is not a game, not some weekend binge gone wrong; it's not something you catch or make happen to yourself. It follows you into the world with your first breath, waiting. It's patient.

The hummingbird caged in your chest makes that first drink dangerous, throwing itself against your ribs until you cannot breath. Anxiety and addiction are old friends: be careful. There is a darkness that will take that hummingbird and shove it's face in a bottle of gin, holding it under that first time until its wings stop moving, until it passes out inside of you. What you feel is stillness, the warmth of the drink in your throat; you don't even know that the bird is nearly dead. You don't know that the bird was your gift to the world once you found the way to free it; you can't even imagine how incomplete the world will be without it.

It won't be long until every day is planned around that first drink; until it's your first thought that your conscious mind thinks in the morning, before you've even opened your eyes. It will define everything about your day. That's how it works.

When you try to escape it, the world is torn open in your head, your mind screams, and everything you feel is amplified, as if the volume on every sadness, every worry, every angry curse has been dialed up as loud as it can go, and the needle registering *damage* has passed the red zone to bury itself beyond sight.

Until you have that drink.

That's what addiction is: it kills the small bird in your chest on purpose; it eliminates your gift to the world.

No one chooses this.

Jimmy was mostly home alone on weekends—drinking. When I went out, I turned away from him sitting there alone. I confess that I did this on purpose. It wasn't so much that I wanted to go out, but sometimes I couldn't bear to be home with him. I was guilty, and I knew it. One night I stopped in the doorway to the family room, which was never occupied by our family, but was the place he sat with a six-pack of beer on the coffee table, and a bottle of vodka stashed under the couch.

I was heartbroken at the sight of him there. I was a terrible sister to leave him like that, and I knew it.

"Hey," I said to him. "There's a party at Stuart Mackenzie's house— do you wanna come?" I didn't say it enthusiastically; there was no smile in my voice. He embarrassed me at parties; he was my brother, the drunk one, the fragile one, the one trying too hard not to fall over.

"Sure," he said.

I tried to smile like I meant it.

The house was dark out front so we parked the car on the edge of the dirt road and went to the back where the music was coming from. I must have walked faster than Jimmy. He stopped to see someone.

"I'll meet you inside," I said, glad he had someone to talk to.

The stairs around the back of the house were lined with people I recognized, smoking, drinking, hanging off the clothesline. I squeezed past them on my way to disappear inside. A stocky, reckless kid called Spencer stood in the doorway, his eyes were bloodshot, his mouth set in a snarl, his head drooping, then bouncing back up.

Someone was holding him up so he didn't fall over.

"Hey Spencer," I said.

He looked blank, drugged.

"He's having a bad trip," someone said. "He's a little feisty."

Burst of male laughter.

'Atta boy, Spence.

Inside I found a group of friends I knew. The music was loud and the room was smoky.

"Hey! You made it." People smiled, someone passed me a drink.

And then it happened.

"Fight, fight, fight!" they shouted. Everyone rushed to the back door. I followed the crowd and like a pack of wild dogs, we moved to the action.

Jimmy, I thought.

"Get out of the way!" I screamed.

I ran.

The night was darker than I ever thought it could be, a crowd of people circled like a lynching, maybe fifty bodies stood in a pack. I pushed my way through.

"What's happening?" I screamed. "What's going on?"

"It's Spencer kicking the shit out of someone."

Then I knew: it was Jimmy.

Spencer was hammering his face into the dirt; my brother's large body trapped underneath him in the mud; Spencer's bloody fist pounding the side of his head, over and over like a hammer driving a spike into a plank.

"Stay back!" the older guys shouted, holding the crowd back like referees, like they were keeping score, like there were rules to follow.

The crowd stood watching, obeying.

I looked around for a shovel, something to hit with, but there was nothing. I leapt over someone's back and clawed my way into the middle. Fists and feet were flying; the slapping, muffled sound of flesh being hit; his body limp.

I grabbed Spencer's hair with both my hands and held on tight. I felt the sweat of his scalp, his skin under my fingernails and I wished for him to die. Spencer swung his elbow back at me but kept pounding, even though my brother wasn't moving.

"Get off him!" I screamed. Someone grabbed me from behind but I was headfirst in the dirt by then with my feet in the air. I kicked as hard as I could and felt my heel connect with someone's face.

The referees decided then they'd seen enough for one night and pulled both of us off the ground. An older guy put Spencer in a headlock and ushered him into the house, like a young hero, some prized boxer who needed a cooldown and a private dressing room.

"Fuck you all!" I yelled. No one cared. No one stayed to help.

With the show over, everyone disappeared inside.

"Jimmy?"

I touched his cheek. He didn't move.

His blood was warm and slippery on my fingertips. I hadn't prayed in a long time, but at that moment I prayed the way desperate people pray. God, please.

"Jimmy. Can you hear me?" I rubbed his back with my hand.

"It's okay, you'll be okay."

I tried to pull his body up onto my lap, to hold him in my arms, but he was too heavy.

And I was too small.

I was smaller and more helpless than I remembered that night.

"I'm okay," he said then, trying to sit up.

"Just lie still for a minute."

I needed time to think.

His hand reached up to touch his head and when he felt the blood, he let out a sob, shivering in the mud. "Oh my God, I'm not okay."

Even in the dark I could see his face swelling, the left side of his head like a balloon about to burst at any moment.

"My glasses," he said.

"It's okay, lie still. I'll find your glasses. Just lie still."

On my knees, in dirt and leaves, I searched the ground, my hands sweeping the driveway with my fingertips, calling back to him.

"It's okay, you'll be okay."

I said this to us both, wishing it to be true.

10

Weeks could pass without incident, or at least without me knowing. I went places I knew he wouldn't be. The night of Ted Anderson's party, *Quiet Riot* was pulsing through the speakers, shaking the Anderson's empty four-car garage. People were smashing beer bottles on the floor, so we all walked ankle deep in broken glass; someone I didn't know came over to me, shouting in my ear. I couldn't hear anything he was saying, but I thought I heard him say something about my brother.

"I can't hear you!" I shouted back. He waved me toward the door so he could talk to me away from the music.

"Are you Jim Young's sister?"

I hesitated. "Yeah, why?"

"Well he's freaking out—he's in the field out there trying to kill somebody's goat or something. He's got a fire going and I think someone called the cops."

"My brother's not even here!"

"I don't know, just thought I'd tell you what I heard."

I looked out across the field and could see an orange glow in the distance. I leaned up against a parked car and wondered what to do.

❧

The field was darker than I expected it to be. There was no trail and the ground was uneven with tall grass and deep sand that slipped beneath my feet. Only the orange glow in the distance was there to guide me. I wondered, as I tripped along, what I would do if it was *not* my brother at the fire, if it was someone else's brother. Then I wondered what I'd do if it *was* my brother. I didn't have a plan.

When I got closer I could see the fire was built in a dip in the ground, sheltered by a circle of small hills of sand. From a distance the fire looked small, but close up I could see the flames reached twenty feet in the air. Someone had built a fire that was meant to burn. Then I heard a strange, struggling, bleating noise. It was a young goat, maybe ten feet from the fire, yanking against a rope around its neck and staked to the ground. The flames were hot and dangerously close.

I couldn't see him, but I could feel him there.

The kid at the party was right.

"Jim?" I said, quietly at first.

There was no answer.

"Jimmy!" I called out into the night, louder than the sound of the crackling fire.

"Where are you?"

The goat cried and kicked. I didn't know what to do.

Once more I called him, "Jim!"

But no one answered.

As I got closer to the flames I could see him then, across the fire from me, on the edge of the darkness, flames flickering between us. He was sitting on a stump with his head in his hands. Maybe crying. Maybe he'd been drinking all night. It was hard to tell.

"Jimmy!" I said to him from across the fire. "It's me."

He looked up, across the fire and straight through me, as if he didn't know who I was, as if I didn't belong there, as if I should go.

"What do you want?" he said, almost expressionless.

It was his eyes; his eyes were different. In his eyes I couldn't see my brother. It was as if my brother was gone and someone else was speaking back to me, someone I didn't know. It was more than alcohol or tiredness or sadness; it was the sly presence of something else.

I didn't have time to think about what was happening, or whether or not this was sensible or real, whether or not my brother had lost his mind. I didn't have time to weigh it all up; my brother was sitting a few feet from me beside a roaring fire he'd built and it looked pretty clear to me that he intended to roast someone's goat. The flames were hot, there were sirens in the night coming closer, and the only thing I was certain of was that my brother was not okay.

The sound of the goat crying out for its life was the only thing that was keeping me sane. It was the only thing that connected me to what I knew had been real: that a boy at a party had told me about a goat, that the goat was real, that this was happening.

"Jim," I said, as I inched closer to him. "Jim, it's me."

His head dropped into his hands and I thought he might pass out. Then I saw the flashing lights across the field out on the highway.

"We have to go now, enough of this." I said it sharply, purposefully, never letting him see me tremble inside. "The cops are coming."

"What are you doing here?" he said then, suddenly, surprised to see me standing there, as if I'd just arrived.

"Jim, we have to go. Someone called the cops and we have to get out of here."

"Okay, okay, sorry, sorry."

"Stand up now and get your head straight," I said. "I have to let this goat go, okay? This is not a game. Do you understand?"

"Of course it's not a fucking game!" He looked straight into my eyes.

I didn't look away. It was my brother looking back at me, then.

I got close to the goat and held it between my knees. It bucked up and down and I struggled to keep it still long enough to loosen the knot. It ran off into the night away from the fire.

"Give me your hand," I said. "We'll go around the back of those houses so no one sees us. Did you drive here?"

He reached into his pocket, pulled out his keys, and handed them to me. I didn't think at all at that moment; I just did what I had to do to get my brother home. We stumbled our way across the field in the dark, crouching through the field. I held on to his hand most of the way, not because I wanted to, but because I could not lose him.

He held on too.

There was a memory in between our fingers that night in the field; it was the memory of a holiday, a day on the ferry in a heavy storm near Vancouver Island, in simpler days. The wind threatened to blow us off the deck that day; it took everything we had to hold on. We were holding each other up, facing something we could not control, something that made us both afraid.

When we got to our house that night, he went straight into his room and shut the door behind him.

"Goodnight," I said to the closed door. He didn't answer.

It was a warm autumn evening and I wasn't tired. I wanted to cry, but I had nothing left. I noticed then, a quiet, sorrowful feeling, grey and cold like a stone, right in the bottom of my chest. It was a feeling as if I missed someone who was never coming home, and I was losing the memory of their face; there was, of course, no one to miss. Not really. Not a real person.

For some reason, for the first time in years, I thought of the key with the blue ribbon. I went into my room, and even though it had been a long time since I'd looked for it, there was a hopeful part of me that wondered if it would be in the same place. I reached up high on the shelf in my room for the dusty Raggedy Ann bank and gave it a little shake. When I peeled off the black rubber stopper and the blue ribbon of the key dangled out, I let tears fill my eyes.

I still had the keys to my brother's car in my pocket and though it must have been well past midnight, the only place in the world I wanted to be right then was with God. The little church was the only place in the world I could think of to go, the only place that could feel like going home.

When I pulled the car into the gravel parking lot, I didn't think about being quiet or invisible. With the images of the field and the fire and the goat swimming in my mind, being quiet didn't seem to matter. I could already imagine the feeling of the red carpet on the floor underneath my cheek. I stepped up to the door and longed to feel it push open the way it always had. I wanted to call out, "I'm home!" and fall into someone's arms.

But as hard as I wished that night, the key with the blue ribbon would not open the door. Even the door handle looked different. Somewhere across the years someone had changed the locks.

Instead, I sat on the stairs of the church for hours that night, smoking all the cigarettes left in the pack. I thought of my brother alone on the stump by the fire. I listened to the crickets hiding in the grass and wished for just one of them to be a firefly. I was faster then, I knew; I could catch a firefly for myself, I was pretty sure.

I would go to my brother, then, as he slept.

I would whisper in his ear, "You can have mine."

And the firefly would light up his dark room.

11

On clear evenings when the sky was thick and black, and my brother and I were little and awake late, my father would make us all go out to look at the night sky. It seemed that every star for miles around had come to hover above our heads. My father would look up, point and say, "There's the Big Dipper," and we would all stare up into the sky, holding still, until my brother said, "There's the Little Dipper!"

It always amazed me that the stars would be able to spin to the same pattern each night, and that my father could always find the same few stars. No matter where we were, on our deck at home or on holidays far away, my family could find those stars.

I never told my family that I couldn't see the Big Dipper. When I looked up into the sky, all I could see was a field of stars. As hard as I squinted, I could never see what they were seeing. My father would point and point; he would tell me to look just near that bright one or just above this dark patch, and finally I would say, "Oh yes, there it is!" because I'd wanted so much to see it too.

When I discovered how easy it was to say it, and how happy they all were when I could finally see it as they did, I felt as if it connected us, as if seeing the same stars in the sky made us belong together.

I wish I had some excuse, some good reason for my behavior at fifteen, sixteen, seventeen. I wish there was some reason—other than the cold fear that grabbed my spine with long thin fingers and coiled around the soft bones of my core, squeezing until I could not breathe—for why I stayed away from him, was busy with friends, came home and slipped upstairs without saying goodnight, even when I knew he was there alone.

Then one day, I passed the door to the family room and glanced in. For a moment, just for that day, the brother I remembered was there. He was eating peanuts, cracking the shells into a bowl, his eyes were clear and young behind his glasses, looking for me.

"Do you want some?" he said, holding the bowl of peanuts out, having nothing else to say to me right then, but wanting not to be alone.

"Sure," I said and sat down to crack open a peanut. There was nothing much to say. Finally the show he was watching came back on.

He could sense me getting ready to stand up and go.

"Have you seen this?" he said. "It's funny, just watch it."

But what he meant was, please stay with me. So I didn't get up that day. I stayed and we sat together, eating every last peanut in the bowl, both of us wishing it was all as simple as this.

Then came the day I would decide to go to him, unafraid. It would change my life forever.

It was spring. My parents were away. Jim was twenty. I could feel it in the room before I even reached the top of the stairs—a thickness in the air, like a current. I hesitated, paused a few stairs from the top, before he could see me.

If I didn't help him, who would? I knew the answer was *nobody*. Would I leave him to it, to whatever had taken hold of him? Could I do that to him? I kept climbing then, each stair taking me closer to what I was most afraid of.

He had a beer can on the table beside him. He was sitting on the floral couch in the living room. He was not drunk; he was the most sober I'd seen him in months. He was wearing a red t-shirt with cutoff sleeves and he sat with his arms crossed, leaning back into the couch, his feet extended in front of him tapping together the way our father's feet used to tap when he was thinking or nervous.

"Jim . . . what's wrong?" I said, feeling something in the room I knew well. This was it. I was going in.

He looked up at me and said nothing for a while.

I didn't move; I just waited.

"Do you really want to know?" he said, not sure why I was standing there, but noticing my eyes, looking at my face to see if I was really asking.

"Yes," I said. "I really want to know," hoping I sounded convincing, hoping he knew how hard I was trying.

"I don't think you can handle it," he said, longing spilling out across his face as he watched for my reaction, gauging the truth of what I'd said.

I sat down on the couch across from him and continued to wait.

And then he began.

"Well," he said, "basically, if you want to know. . . ." He stopped, took a breath for courage. "My body is a harbor for demons and there's nothing I can do about it." He smiled at me, the way people smile when they've just confessed the end of everything, when they've laid it all out and they've got nothing left to lose.

He said nothing else, reached for his beer can and discovered it was empty but didn't get up to get another one.

I said nothing, wondering if this was a test, wondering if he was about to laugh out loud instead. I tried not to react at all at first, to keep my voice even and calm.

"What do you mean?" I said. "What do you mean a harbor for demons?"

He thought for a minute before he answered. "Like they live inside of me—not all the time, but when they need to."

"What makes you think that?" I said slowly, inviting him to talk so I could think. He'd just said it straight out. I had no idea how to react; I had absolutely no idea what to say.

"I don't *think* it, I *know* it." He tapped his feet together and then stood up to go to the kitchen.

"And the worst part is," he called from the fridge, "I can't ever get rid of them. Because of what they'd do to *you*."

"What are you *talking* about . . . ?" My voice betrayed me, cracking.

"Forget it, okay? Just fucking forget it." I heard him rummaging around in the kitchen.

Then the back door opened to the deck.

I knew I was getting it wrong, but I couldn't have this conversation any other way. I was struggling just to stay in the room. I thought of running down the stairs while he was outside and driving away. I thought of getting my fishing knife and hiding it in my pocket. I knew that it had taken a lot of courage for him to say what he'd said; I could see it on his face.

I got up then and went to the back door. He'd poured himself a drink of something stronger and was sitting on the picnic table, sipping. In the dimness of the backlight, I could see the outline of his shoulders, slouching the way he used to when we sat together to watch the robins.

I opened the screen door and walked to him. He didn't look up. I didn't say anything at all; I just sat beside him on the table. The night was clear and cold.

"You don't fucking get it," he said.

"I'm trying to get it, Jimmy, I am *really* trying here!" My voice was edgy. What more could I say or do? Honestly, it's not every day your brother tells you he's got demons living inside him; I didn't have much left.

There was silence for a few minutes. Maybe longer, I didn't keep track. It was like a nightmare in slow motion, the kind you hope to wake up from. He breathed out heavily, drank back the rest of his drink, and stared out to the street, maybe not caring if I even listened.

"Basically," he said, "if I try to get rid of them, they'll hurt you, maybe even kill you. Do you understand that? They've tried before."

What do you say to that? When you're seventeen?

What can you even think?

I said nothing.

I stared out at the street.

"You don't believe me, do you?" he said, shaking his head.

I could see he understood that he was all alone, more alone than he'd ever been.

"I do believe you," I said, but my voice wavered. He would notice this.

"Okay, I'm *trying* to believe you." I just sat there, not knowing what else to do. I had no idea what to believe.

"I don't really know enough about it," I said finally.

"What more is there to know?" he said. "That's just my life. That's the way it is. I'm fucked. There's nothing anyone can do about it."

At that moment, I vowed in my heart to believe him, to help him. "I do believe you, Jim. I'm going to figure out how to help you."

He turned to look at me, and I didn't look away. I stared into his eyes then, promising him. He shrugged, brushing it off, pretending it didn't matter, but when his eyes filled with water, he looked away. I wish I'd put my arms around him at that moment. I wish I'd hugged him and rocked him and let him sob in my arms.

I stared up at the night sky. It was velvety black. A field of stars had gathered to hover over our heads and that night I saw the Big Dipper, clear as the street lights, right where it had always been.

12

The darkness that had crept inside my brother was not something I could discuss with anyone. Initially because I was afraid, but later, when I'd thought about it night after night, I knew it was a secret he'd trusted me with. I didn't see it at the time, of course, but I held on to that secret, selfishly. It was the intimacy of that secret that I clung to; it connected me to the brother I'd lost. I knew my parents wouldn't be of any help. They moved through each day somewhere on the other side of the glass, chained to their own unhappiness.

Maya Angelou once said, "There is no greater agony than bearing an untold story inside of you."

When I knew my father was dying, I rushed to finish the first draft of my book. I would read it to him, I'd decided, even before it was polished. Why hadn't I explained it all sooner, while he was well? Perhaps I could have given him some years of peace. He deserved to know. I would finally explain the secrets I'd kept from him that might have made a difference. It was time.

I began to read the messy draft from the beginning, being careful to read a few pages at a time when he was awake long enough to concentrate. As I got closer to the pages that captured the secrets I'd kept, I began to panic but I forced myself to keep going.

When I'd finally read to him the first pages about the darkness, I looked up from the page and saw him there in the chair across the room with his head in his hands. He was crying.

"Dad, what's wrong?" I said, but I knew. I was an idiot. Why had I done this to him now? What made me think he'd needed to know this now, in the last days of his life?

"I'm sorry, Dad," I sobbed. "I'm so sorry." I tried to explain. "I should have told you sooner, I should have talked to you. . . ."

He lifted his hand to stop me, trying to get control of himself to speak.

"I knew!" he shouted through his tears. "Oh God, I knew, I knew, I just didn't know what to do!"

I was stunned.

"You knew?"

"Yes, I knew. I knew there was something terrible going on inside of him, some kind of evil, but I couldn't face it." He cried harder. "I just didn't know what the hell to do. I didn't have anything left."

❦

We all knew. We just didn't know what to do.

So at seventeen, I began the journey to find help for my brother, to keep the promise I'd made to him that night on the deck, that I'd find help.

But where on earth do you begin? Where do you go for help with demons? I knew the Bible well enough to know it had passages on this kind of thing, stories that might confirm whether or not this was possible, if what my brother was saying might be right.

I scoured the public library for anything I could find on demons and demonology, surprised to find a small collection on ritualistic worship practices, Satanism, and accounts of the demonized. They all seemed to confirm that yes, it was entirely possible, that Jimmy could be right. But there were no solutions. Why was that? In the end I turned to the little white Bible on my shelf. But where do you begin, at seventeen, with a book containing hundreds of thousands of words in the tiniest of print written on pages so thin I feared they would tear as I turned them?

Walk by faith, not by sight. God has chosen the foolish things of the world to confound the wise. Watch and pray lest you fall into temptation. Trust in the Lord in with all of your heart and lean not on your own understanding. He that doubteth is damned.

He that doubteth is damned.

Would I, through my doubts, be damned? Would I take my brother down with me?

Then I came across it. There, in the back of my Bible, was a kind of index. I was careful not to damage the clover still tucked in the creases as I scanned the pages until I saw one that listed the *Miracles of Jesus*. There was a section called *Power Over Unclean Spirits* that had the notation *Matthew 8:28* written beside it. When I found the section in Matthew, I read it carefully:

> *And when he was come to the other side . . . there met him two possessed with devils, coming out of the tombs . . .*
>
> *So the devils besought him saying,*
>
> *"If thou cast us out, suffer us to go away into the herd of swine."*
> *And he said unto them, "Go."*

Yes, I thought, this is it, this is what must be done. The devils must go. I read on:

> *And when they were come out, they went into the herd of swine: and behold the whole herd of swine ran violently down a steep place into the sea, and perished in the waters.*
>
> *And they that kept them fled, and went their ways into the city, and told everything, and what was befallen to the possessed of the devils.* (KJV)

I read the section four times, slowly.

The possessed of the devils. I tried to breathe, to pay attention to each word.

My mouth was dry, my head ached. I would need help.

I didn't know the new minister at church very well, but I was sure it was his job to help me. He was new to the church, but he was, after all, an expert in this field. His name was Reverend McMurphy. He was a nervous man who pretended that he wasn't nervous. He once told my father that he preferred private prayer and Bible study to working with people. His sermons were mostly reflections on his weekly experiences in nature, out kayaking or hiking in the mountains. It was no secret in our house that Reverend McMurphy's sermons irritated my father. "What kind of a minister talks about the hours he spends hiking all week to a church full of working guys who have sweated all week to make a dollar—which they are then asked to give to him, I might add—on the only day of the week they get off? And not only do they have to sit for an hour listening to him talk about his boat trips, but they've got to pay him for it!" my father had complained.

I stared at the number for Reverend McMurphy in the phone book for a long time before I dialed it. I had no idea what to say but I knew I had to do it.

"It's Heather Young," I said when he answered. "I'd like to make an appointment to talk to you."

He stammered, wasn't sure what his schedule was, could I be more specific?

"Not really," I said. "I need to talk to you about this in person."

Reluctantly, once he'd found his appointment book and checked to see if he was available that week, he agreed.

The next Wednesday after school, I borrowed my parents' car and went to my appointment at the little church by the ski hill. It had been a long time. When I pulled into the parking lot, Reverend McMurphy's Subaru was there with two kayaks strapped to the roof.

The church did not, that day, have that warm, coming-home feeling that I had imagined the night I sat on the steps of the church listening to the crickets. It felt official. The church was cold, even though it was May.

I wondered if Reverend McMurphy knew where the thermostat was for the heat, but I decided against mentioning it.

I made my way up the stairs and into the sanctuary. He had the door to the little office propped open with a chair. I'd never seen inside the office before; it was the one room that was always locked. I'd imagined it to have thick curtains and a cross on the wall; I'd imagined him waiting for me with his white minister's collar on.

Instead, Reverend McMurphy was dressed in a thick wool sweater and hiking boots. The room was simple with a small desk and two chairs. There were no books or crosses, nothing that made it seem like part of a church. And even though it was May, last year's calendar hung on the wall open at September with an autumn forest scene. He stood up when I came around the corner.

"Heather, hi!" he said, a little too enthusiastically, coming over to shake my hand but changing his mind at the last second and reaching instead to hold the edge of the door. He motioned for me to sit down in one of the chairs. We chatted for a second about the warming weather; he asked about school and what my plans were for the next year. Then we got down to business; it began to feel like an interview.

"So, what can I do for you?" he said.

I pulled my white Bible out of my bag where I'd marked the page at Matthew. "I was wondering about demons," I said. "I found this part in the Bible about demons, Jesus casting demons into a herd of swine, and I just wondered what you thought of that."

He looked relieved, smiled easily, then nearly laughed.

"Oh, well, that's easy. I wasn't sure what you were after, but it's a theological question, which is good! It shows you're thinking."

I smiled, waited for him to talk.

"Basically that's a reference to what we would understand today as more of a metaphorical evil. It's not anything to worry about, that's for sure. Culturally we live in such a different day that biblical references like these can be confusing."

I had no idea what he meant, but I nodded because I could tell he wanted me to have understood.

"Does that make sense?" he asked.

"I guess so." I thought for a minute. "So is this a true story or not?"

What was it that made me completely turn this subject over to Reverend McMurphy, to sit myself down and wait for him to deliver the answers? It must have been more than my age. Perhaps it was the comfort I found in letting someone think for me. Or perhaps the task of understanding what was contained in those magical pages seemed impossible. I did not yet want to understand those pages; I wanted answers, plain and simple. I wanted the ease of slipping under the guidance of a kind of wizard who ought to know, who had been trained to know, someone who would carry the weight of the truth.

"Well, truth is a very subjective thing. And truth can look different at different times."

I nodded again.

What I wanted to say was, please help me, I think my brother might be possessed by demons, and I don't know what to do. I tried one more time.

"So do you think there are demons or not?" I asked him.

"To be honest, it's not an area I know much about. It falls outside of my area of expertise, but I do think there are influences of evil that evidence themselves as greed, anger, sinfulness, that kind of thing. It's really nothing to worry about."

"Oh," I said.

"Does that answer your question?" he said, looking at his watch.

"I guess so." I didn't know what else to say. "So people don't believe in demons today . . . ?" I clarified.

"Well, there are some theological positions that would very much believe in demonic forces in that way, some churches put more emphasis on that, but it's not common in the United Church. The United Church takes a more academic approach to passages like the one in Matthew you've found there."

"Really?" my interest sparked. "Do you mean other churches here?"

"Oh yes," he went on, "People have very different views about difficult passages like this one. Yes, even here in Prince George there are some cracker-jacks out there who believe all kinds of crazy things," he chuckled. I didn't like the way he said *cracker-jacks*.

I nodded.

"Is there anything else I can help you with?" he said. "I hate to rush you, we're just off kayaking this afternoon for a couple of days, but if you have more questions we could make another appointment."

I told him I didn't have anymore questions.

I didn't know then that this would be the first of nine such visits, to nine different churches to speak to nine different clergy, looking for answers. I didn't know that Baptists and Catholics and Presbyterians and Anglicans would, in the end, seem very much the same from my chair across the desk. I didn't know it would take dozens of appointments and phone calls for me to come to the realization that the Church was uncomfortable when it didn't have the answers. When the Church was stumped, I watched it skirt around the edges, ducking in behind a brochure that outlined the steps to salvation, forcing a smile and checking the time. I didn't know I would eventually look at my collection of pamphlets and brochures and scraps of paper with contact phone numbers for prayer chains or ladies' Bible study groups and weep, great tears of despair rolling down my cheeks.

13

The only thing more welcome than a problem that solves itself, is a problem that turns out not to be one, thank God. We do it so easily when we have to; we close the curtains, turn on a movie, and bring on the popcorn. With the curtains closed, you can almost convince yourself there's no such thing as darkness.

My brother seemed happier. Months had passed without incident. He *did* seem happier; I'm sure he did. He was painting a lot, mostly wildlife. The rage in his artwork had disappeared. The demons and darkness that once forced their way on to the canvas had gone.

He'd been dating a lovely girl I knew from high school band. Her name was Uta. She was a year older than he was, quiet and plain, timid like a soft, grey mouse. She seemed to make him happy. Together they joined a bird watcher's club, hiked the trails around town armed with binoculars and packed lunches, and drank German beer with her family.

Perhaps everything really would be all right.

I'd started to laugh with him again; we laughed together as we hadn't laughed in a very long time. It was the kind of laughing that made you lose your balance, a reassuring kind of laughter.

It seemed enormously difficult, wasteful even, to think about it then. Why spoil things?

The conversation we'd had on the deck that night, the demons and the darkness, it all seemed to belong to a shattered night in another universe. It belonged to different people, not to my brother and me. I forced those thoughts out of my head when they crept in, in a superstitious way; I worried I might summon up the nightmare again, just when everything was healthy and normal.

Though I didn't acknowledge it at the time, I felt myself pull away from Jim when Uta became part of his life. It seemed as if someone else had come to carry the load. I was tired. I was afraid of what I knew, but also what I didn't know. So I did not carry my end of the load. Instead, I set it on the ground at her feet and felt myself begin to walk away.

When they were engaged a few months later, I confess it seemed to be the chance to slip the cuffs off of my wrists without anyone noticing.

Then one night, a few months in, it began to be clear that I was not free. Jimmy was out with Uta at a pub with friends. My mother went to bed, and my dad must have been watching television and waiting up for Jim. I'd gone to bed early.

At 11:04 I woke up in a sweat, startled. My heart began to thud inside my chest, beating against the inside of my ribs like a fist, waking me from a deep sleep. I blinked, listening.

Something was wrong. I could feel it.

Something was terribly wrong but I didn't know what.

I waited.

I stood up and looked out my window. His car was not in the driveway; it was still early for Jim on a Saturday night. My heart settled but I felt uneasy. I lay back down and closed my eyes.

As I pulled the blankets up around my shoulders, I heard his car pull into the driveway. I heard the emergency brake twist on, then two car doors opening and one slamming shut. I relaxed a little. Uta was with him. Then I heard her voice, unnaturally loud, shouting at Jim.

"Just come in the house and stop talking!" I heard her say. "Jim, get in the house!" Her voice broke, she was crying. I got out of bed and went downstairs.

When I opened the front door, I could see Jim in the car, Uta was standing by the front door, calling to him and crying.

"What happened?" I said.

"He's being so weird!" She looked scared.

"What happened?" I needed to know what she knew.

"He just started acting weird, and I'm scared of him!" She was shaking, starting to cry more intentionally, but I had no patience for what she felt.

"Uta, I need to know exactly what happened. It's really important; please just tell me what happened."

"I don't know!" she snapped at me. "He wasn't even drinking that much and then he just started acting weird." Jim had his eyes closed and his head pressed back against the car seat, the interior light was on because his door was open and one leg was out of the car on the driveway. He looked stiff but asleep.

"When, Uta?" I asked her, "When did this happen?"

"I don't know, we were at a party and then he said he had to go home right away. I was driving so he went out to the car, and I finished talking to someone. On the way home he was trying to crawl out the window and he was saying all these terrible things!" She looked shocked and embarrassed. "Oh my God, it was awful, Heather. I need him to get out of the car. I need to go home." She started sobbing.

Just then my dad appeared at the door.

"What's the matter?" he said when he saw her crying.

"He really scared me. I have to go home. He won't get out of the car."

I felt my face flush. I'd never mentioned anything to her about Jim. I'd hoped she knew; I thought they would have talked about it. Surely to God they would have at least *talked* about it, wouldn't they?

My dad went to get Jim out of the car. He shook him and took his arm to help him out of the car. Uta wouldn't look at him. When he'd gone in the mudroom door, she got in the car and drove away.

At that moment, I knew she would not be able to help him. Not ever.

Who *could* help him? How can you help someone who has a problem no one understands? I'd left it too late to ask my father for help. And there I was, believing I was the only person in the world who knew how dark it was inside of Jimmy, tucking him away like a bird in a box in my closet, hoping he'd get better.

I shut the front door and started to walk upstairs when I heard my dad telling him to settle down.

"Jim, take it easy!" They were in the coatroom at the back door. It sounded like a scuffle. I opened the door to the hallway; my dad looked small compared to my brother. I hadn't noticed that before.

"What's wrong?" I said to my dad.

"He's just been drinking too much, that's all," my dad said.

"No!" Jim shouted. "You don't understand."

"Quiet, your mother is sleeping!"

"I want to talk to my sister."

My dad looked back at me.

I stared at him. What I wanted to say was, please don't leave me with him, not like this. Please. Instead I said nothing. Jimmy turned, went into the bathroom, and shut the door. I watched my dad's face, to see if he understood any of this. He didn't seem to.

"Too much to drink," he said. I could see him thinking about all the times he'd had too much to drink as a youngster: bar fights, drunk tanks—this, too, would pass. Was he thinking, at that point, that something might be very wrong with his son?

"Don't stay too long talking, okay?" he said to me, shaking his head as he went upstairs.

I could not explain it to him right then. Not then, not in the middle of the night. I stood outside the door of the bathroom and thought; I leaned up against the frame staring at the wood grain.

And then I heard it.

It was as clear as if I was in the same room.

There was a growling noise like a dog with his teeth bared coming from the bathroom, like a wolf standing over its kill, deep and throaty; it was a warning. At that moment the image I had in my mind was of something terrible standing over my brother, backing him into the corner, about to kill him. I hit the door with my palm.

"Jim! Open the door!" I hit the door harder. "Jimmy!"

I don't know why my dad didn't hear and come back.

I reached for the handle and the door opened.

There was no dog in the bathroom; instead there was my brother staring at himself in the mirror, his face three inches away from his reflection, growling. His neck was veined and muscled; it was strangely thick with the skin pulled so tight it looked as if it might split open.

"Jim!"

He turned to look at me, but it was not my brother looking back at me.

"Jim, stop it!" I prayed this wasn't real, that it wasn't happening.

I backed slowly out of the bathroom and into the hallway toward the mudroom. I couldn't see him anymore but I could hear him, low growling, moving around the bathroom, bumping up against the towel rack. I backed myself into the hallway. I should have opened the mudroom door and ran, but I was too frightened to turn my back. I leaned up against the wall and prayed, Dear God, help.

At that moment I felt God close beside me in a way I hadn't in years.

It was God all right; right there in the mudroom hallway, standing beside me, waiting.

Jim came out of the bathroom then; his neck was swollen and muscled; his eyes were not my brother's. They were the eyes of the person who'd built the fire in the field. He came toward me slowly, staring as if seeing through me to the wall behind my head. I pressed myself against the wall; my heart was a fist in my chest, in my throat.

Then, quite suddenly, something slipped around me, like some peace that passes all understanding, as if I was inside something safe and clear. There was nothing visible but I felt it; thin and strong and transparent, the way it might feel to be inside a glass Christmas bulb that cannot be broken. I cannot describe the sensation any other way.

And strangely, my fear was gone too, just like that. I could breathe again. I felt God right there but not beside me anymore. Instead it seemed God was somehow, crazily, in my hand, of all places, warm and smooth like a small blue egg from a robin's nest, tucked in the center of my palm. I was not afraid. I lifted my right hand and held my palm up toward my brother and closed my eyes.

I don't know why I did this, but it made him stop coming toward me.

When I opened my eyes, he was backing up slowly, until he was pressed up against the opposite wall. I closed my eyes and held my hand out toward his chest. I stepped toward him then, my hand seemed to reach to his chest on its own.

I knew that I needed to place my hand on his chest in order to reach him. When my hand came close, I felt a strong magnetic repulsion forcing my hand away. Perhaps it was my own fear, but for a moment I couldn't force my hand against his chest.

I didn't look up at his face. He was 6'2"; I stared straight ahead at his chest. I heard him breathing anxiously, sharply.

I held steady and lifted my left hand carefully in behind to push the right one forward; I closed my eyes.

Then the pressure between us seemed to ease quite suddenly, as if the air had been let out.

When I touched him, there was nothing miraculous, nothing magical, no lightning bolts. When I touched him, I simply felt his chest and the white button on his shirt pocket beneath my hand. I felt his breathing and the life in his body underneath that button. I looked up into his face; his neck was soft, his eyes were my brother's.

I took my hand away, the glass Christmas bauble was gone, my father opened the door.

"Jim, it's time to get into bed," he said.

"Yup, I'm going," my brother said. He seemed quiet, a little confused, but not drunk.

That night the rules about my whole world changed. There *were* dark places that people didn't believe in, that Reverend McMurphy and the church ministers and my parents didn't take any notice of. There was a dangerous, dark edge to the world, sharp as a knife—and it didn't matter whether or not I understood it. It didn't care whether or not I *believed* in it. It was there just the same.

I watched that dark edge slide across my brother's throat that night, then quietly slip away and disappear. I was terrified for us both.

The next day was ordinary.

The sun came up like any other day.

It was Sunday but no one went to church.

I had a bowl of cereal for breakfast.

Jim mowed the lawn, painted in the basement.

My mother made spare ribs and invited Uta for dinner.

My father paid bills in his office.

When Uta came over in the evening, she still looked perplexed.

"You were being so weird!" she said to Jim when we sat out on the back deck. "Don't do that; it got me really scared."

He laughed, shaking his head, the way people do when they're remembering the night before, having tripped down the stairs or walked around with no pants on.

"I don't know what happened . . . too many beers." He held her hand and laughed, shrugging.

She slapped him playfully and leaned up against his shoulder.

I got up to go inside.

Was I losing my mind? I looked for his eyes, for some sense of what was real.

When he turned his face to me, his eyes were not embarrassed or afraid.

They stared straight back at me, holding steady, saying, Do you see? Do you believe me now?

I looked away and went inside.

The next Sunday I went to church by myself. Reverend McMurphy was away and a guest speaker gave the sermon. He told a story from the Bible about a Good Shepherd who had a hundred sheep; when one of them was lost, he left the ninety-nine others to go and find the lost one.

I didn't pay attention to what the passage was supposed to mean, all I could think about was that one lost sheep.

That night, in the time between sleep and awake, I saw the Ark in my mind again. Only this time the Good Shepherd was inside the boat eating with the family.

He got up to check on the sheep.

When he'd counted them all, he stopped and looked around the boat. When he turned his face toward me, I could see he was thinking deeply; he was puzzled, nervous.

Then he went back to the beginning and counted again, his eyes searching the dark corners in the back of the boat. Was he frantic?

I saw him shake his head. It was true; one was missing.

The Good Shepherd did not finish his rice; he didn't stop to explain.

He went straight up the ladder to the window and looked out at the storm.

"Jimmy!" he called out into the storm. "Where are you?"

And when he could hear nothing above the sound of the wind and the rain, he shouted, "Be still!"

But what do you do then, if the storm will not be stilled?

What then?

The Good Shepherd stared down at the dark waters, thinking, scanning the water with his eyes.

"Jimmy!" he called out again.

Then he climbed up on the wooden railing and dove into the black night of the sea.

14

*L*unatic is a word that has its roots in "lunar," stemming from an ancient belief that people were struck mad by the moon—"moonstruck," people used to say.

"Don't look at the moon, you'll go crazy." In the sixteenth century, "crazy" meant that something was full of cracks and flaws—*crazed*. Aren't we all full of cracks and flaws? The moon watches the earth from its place in the sky, sweeping slowly round the planet every twenty-eight days. The moon sees the people who walk in darkness, even if we don't.

Every forty seconds, someone on the planet takes his own life. While we're watching our favorite show on cable, four people kill themselves during the commercial break. Every year one million people commit suicide.

The moon watches from the sky.

If darkness is a being, it kills like a python, lurking just out of sight, waiting for the right moment. When it strikes from some silent place, it grabs hard with its teeth but it's not the teeth that will kill you. When a python strikes, it uses its teeth to hold on to the flesh and coils around the body, squeezing. It is a patient killer. Each time you exhale, it squeezes harder, until at last not one more breath is possible. My brother belonged to the moon, not the sun. Perhaps we both did.

I decided to leave the little United Church by the ski hill. I left the felt board stories and the dead people who didn't matter, the warm velvet curtain behind the cross, the stairs I'd smoked cigarettes on, the key on the blue ribbon, and Don McMurphy standing by his kayaks.

I drove slowly past Emmanuel United on my way downtown to a new church that first Sunday morning. I knew what I had to do; I needed answers. Why did I feel such an ache inside of me? I wanted to wave or stop to say good-bye, to stand out front and explain myself on the steps. But of course there was no one to notice I'd gone. So I stared at the steps, swallowed the great longing that rose in my throat, and kept driving.

That first Christmas at the Evangelical Free Church, the Bouwman sisters were lined up on stage singing Christmas hymns as the congregation found their seats, as if they'd slipped down from heaven on the strings of stars reaching to the twenty-foot Christmas tree behind them. The girls were lined up and glowing like candles on a cake: one—two—three—four—five. Their trained voices in a complex harmony, as effortless as breathing, a family choir, gentle, blonde beauties singing every hymn by heart, their hands folded neatly in their laps or clasped gracefully in front of them as if to say, we are at home here.

No one needed to tell me that the Bouwman sisters had been born into this church family. No one needed to say that the church had watched the girls' Sunday dresses being passed down from one to the next as each grew taller and the hem came above the knee. No one needed to tell me that the girls had served tea in the church basement after every special service, that they played skipping games on the long rope after evening Bible study. No one needed to tell me that every church mother with a son wanted him, one day, to marry a Bouwman sister.

And no one needed to tell me that first Christmas, when I'd slipped in the back pew, that my clothes smelled like cigarettes, that my eyeliner was too thick, that my jacket was too black. And it was clear to all from that moment, without anyone needing to ask me, that I'd never learned to skip or sew or stitch or serve tea or memorize Scripture.

I tried to imagine my brother there at the Evangelical Free Church, but I could not.

In his spare time, my father was a prospector. Perhaps, in the beginning, he believed he would find the Mother Lode; he never did. I don't think he was unhappy about this; I think he came to enjoy, instead, walking in the forest in search of it.

In the beginning, I think, my father set out with every intention of finding gold. But afterward, once the search itself became what he needed, once this journey offered him the luxury of escape, the gold must have stopped mattering. Like my father, I set out on a quest that would stop mattering.

In the spring, I joined a Bible study group at the Evangelical Free Church on Wednesday evenings. It didn't take long to surface, that longing to be part of it all. If this really is the way to God, I thought, I want to belong the way the Bouwman sisters do. I was no longer there for just answers; I wanted in. This didn't take long either. I was still the girl who had mastered smoke rings; I was still good at party tricks.

"Bring your Bible if you have one," the pastor had said.

"I have one!" I told him, my voice too eager to please. The little white Bible was on the bookshelf behind my door, as beautiful as I'd remembered it. Even the gold zipper shone and the glass bauble with the mustard seed still felt like magic in my hand.

"Turn to Ephesians Chapter 2," the group leader said.

I unzipped my Bible carefully and started to turn the pages slowly, from Genesis.

I felt the girl beside me staring, shaking her head. She was younger than me, too young to know better.

"It's in the New Testament," she said, reaching for my Bible and flipping the pages fast until she found the place. Why did I let her take it from my hands?

Then, as if in slow motion, as if time itself had frozen inside of me, before I could stop it, I watched her bend my Bible back on itself, almost in half, crushing the stiff spine until it snapped. And at that moment I felt a snap deep inside of me, as if something sacred had broken in two, up under my ribs.

When she passed the book back to me, a dried clover fell out of the pages and spun softly to the carpet like a helicopter seed.

"What's that?" she said, her nose wrinkling.

I stared at the green leaves on the carpet, remembering. For a long sorrowful moment, I remembered it all. I didn't answer her. I had no idea what to say. Even if I could, I would never explain what it meant, at that moment, to see the clover there on the floor.

"It's clover," I said finally, not looking at her.

"Weird," she said. "Why do you have weeds in your Bible?"

I sat back in my chair, frozen inside my own silence, taking in the sounds around me: opening prayers murmuring from clusters of people gathered in the corners of the room, a guitar being tuned. I stared at the clover on the floor and then I answered her.

"I really don't know," I heard myself say.

It was the truest thing I could have said.

By the summer I was twenty, I was a new creation. The old had mostly gone. I memorized Scripture, led the youth group, and made friends in every proper evangelical church in town. I'd learned to say the right phrases at the right time—"Thank you, Jesus. Yes, Lord!"—and to lift my hands when we sang, to pray to Jesus instead of to God. I sang in the Christmas service with the Bouwman sisters and volunteered at Ness Lake Bible Camp.

I had devotions every morning, went to outreach meetings on Tuesdays, Bible study on Wednesday nights, ladies' prayer group on Thursdays after class, ministry planning meetings on Friday afternoons, and church twice on Sundays.

I had made my way in.

When I sang those words, *I once was lost but now am found*, I felt them inside of me. It didn't matter if it was true or not. What I felt was a sense of safety. This is how it feels to be "found," I thought. There was no room for the moon. When you are living in a sunny world of Sundays, you don't notice the people who walk at night with the moon at their side.

But this is how you first discover you're lost:

You begin to take notice of small things at first; small enough to be no big deal, but noticeable.

At the Women's Ministry afternoon, you smile when a woman holds out some wool and a metal crochet hook. "You'll have to learn to crochet," she says.

"Oh, it's not really my thing," you say to her, politely.

When everyone stops, looks up from their needles, staring coldly across the table at you, you reach for the wool. No one says a word.

And then there are moments that make you want to run, but you don't, not yet—moments that claw at that sunny, Sunday feeling, that terrify you more than the night you left behind.

You are a helper in the grade one Sunday School class, working with Mrs. Campbell, who has been teaching Sunday School for thirty years. Tiffany is six. She sometimes comes to Sunday School with her sister, often in her pajamas or wearing clothes that smell of urine. Tiffany is not friendly or pudgy or cute. She has thin wrists and narrow eyes that are puffy with tiredness and clumps of yellow sleep in the corners. She says *dammit* when she drops her pencil on the floor and says it again when no one notices.

One day someone—perhaps Tiffany—colors with purple marker on one of the doll's faces.

When Mrs. Campbell notices the markings, she shouts out her name: "Tiffany! What have you done?"

Tiffany leaps right in without missing a beat, staring at the doll in exaggerated disbelief, no remorse, no guilt, just living the moment.

Tiffany grabs the doll.

"Look at you, you naughty baby!" she yells. "Look at what you've done! I'm going to spank your ass good and hard."

Mrs. Campbell snatches the doll from Tiffany and shouts, "Go out in the hall this minute, Tiffany! Go out of this room right now and stand with your nose against the wall until I get out there! Do you hear me?"

The other children are silent.

Tiffany opens the door, runs down the hall and up the stairs. She does not take her jacket or her coloring papers.

Mrs. Campbell shrugs.

Tiffany does not come back to Sunday School.

Not ever.

You stop the singing in your heart.

You cannot sing those words anymore.

You go one night to a Healing and Deliverance evening at the Pentecostal church. It's a church you haven't visited yet. You go alone, thinking of Jimmy.

You arrive at a few minutes after 7 p.m. You don't want to be early, standing alone in a corner. You've never been to a Pentecostal church, but you are prepared for it to be different. The singing is well underway when you arrive, people are dancing at the front of the church and lifting their hands in the air as if they are at a concert. You sit in the balcony, not judging, just thinking.

When the speaker invites people to come forward, a crowd moves toward the stage, forming long lines on either side, longing to be touched by the speaker's hands. And one by one, the speaker prays over people, touching them on the forehead and pushing them back gently until they fall backward into the arms of the helpers, signifying release and acceptance of God's healing and deliverance. The lineup grows.

In the lineup on the left-hand side you see a girl you recognize from high school. Her name is Charlene. She was a few years older than you. At Kelly Road School she hadn't had any friends and most people didn't speak to her; she ate lunch alone in the band room. People moved seats if she sat near them. They told stories about her that you'd tried to believe weren't true, stories about what she did with her father. She didn't wash very often. She wore the same grey sweatshirt nearly everyday.

Only at her graduation do you remember seeing her wear anything but that grey sweatshirt. She wore a pale yellow gown that she had pinned smaller in the back so it didn't fall down and draped a white sweater over her shoulders to hide the pins.

And here she is, all these years later, at the end of the lineup at the Pentecostal church, waiting to be healed, waiting to be delivered from Satan's power. When she gets closer to the front of the line, the girls in front of you notice her, whispering too loudly.

"Oh my God, look who's there!" one says.

When Charlene reaches the man with the powerful hands, he lifts his hands, as he's done all evening, and then stops and stands back. Is he startled by something unexpected?

He moves toward her then, slowly, whispering in tongues you think, and then she falls, much too soon. She just falls over. No helpers catch her. She hits the ground hard.

You can't see what's happening then, if she's hit her head, if she's unconscious, but the helpers rush around her then, forming a praying circle, a group speaking in tongues and crying out, the powerful man bending over her. There's a shrieking and screaming, a terrible piercing sound, an exhaling screech like a screamer firecracker that doesn't seem to end.

The people pray and shake around her, but you can't see what's happening in the middle of the circle. The girl with the pinned graduation gown is lying somewhere on the ground. The screaming goes on. The circle grabs her by the arms and legs and carries her to the middle of the stage where they can all reach her better to touch her body as they pray. The guest speaker shouts orders and lifts his arms to heaven dramatically, summoning the power of God.

This goes on for some time. The people in the lineup start checking their watches, deciding to go now that there's been a delay. They sneak out the doors to start their cars.

When the screaming has stopped, you make your way down the stairs, not knowing what else to do. The snow has begun to fall outside. The parking lot is emptying. You stand in the foyer staring at posters for a while, thinking.

In a few minutes Charlene comes striding out of the sanctuary, wearing her Kelly Road School jacket, all these years later. You catch her eye on the way past and smile.

You want to ask her if she's okay, if what happened up there was "*a deliverance.*" You want to say you're sorry for the way people treated her in high school. You want to say a lot of things. But you don't.

Hi, is all you manage to say. Nothing more.

You can tell she recognizes you.

She smiles back.

She does not say hello, but instead shrugs in your direction, smiling sadly then, as if to say, Oh well, I guess that's it then.

She pushes open the door and steps out into the night.

As you warm your car, you sit listening to the radio while the back window defrosts. On the sidewalk, walking with the same stride you remember, wearing her Kelly Road jacket, is Charlene, the girl who has just been delivered from demons.

She is still alone, walking with the moon at her side.

15

So it sounds like you're disappointed with God," the pastor said when I tried, that first time, to articulate what I was feeling.

"No," I thought for a minute. "Not with God."

At least I didn't think so.

"I guess, if I'm disappointed, it's with the Church, not with God."

"That's a strong thing to say," he cautioned me.

Was he telling me to step back in line?

"I guess I just expected it to be about more than this, more than Bible study groups and coffee sessions, whether or not we should have disposable communion cups and who gets to choose the color of the Christmas tea napkins."

I held the image of Christ on the cross in my mind, nails in his hands, the darkness taking him. *Thy will be done.*

"Shouldn't there be more to it than this?" I said. "Is this it? Is this what the cross was for?"

He nodded, not agreeing, but just buying time while he thought.

"You should consider baptism," he said. "It makes all the difference, to make that public commitment."

I smiled and nodded, not agreeing, but buying time.

"I'll think about it."

I'd been baptized as a baby. I was pretty sure that wasn't what was missing.

I didn't know then that important theological debates across the centuries about infant baptism had long ago reached an historical impasse. For some, the baptism of an infant is a deeply faith-filled expression of a belief that acknowledges the helplessness of humanity before God. It professes that we are never capable of earning God's favor, that we are welcomed like crying, struggling infants into God's loving hands. For others, baptism is a rite of passage, a public expression of faith, a step of deeper commitment taken only when one is ready to make that choice.

"Have you given your life to Jesus and asked him to be the Lord of your life?"

"Of course I have."

"Are you embarrassed?"

"No, that's not it." Was he trying to *shame* me?

Then again, I had nothing to lose.

There were a few of us up for baptism that June. It was held on Father's Day at Ness Lake Bible Camp; the lake was still cold.

"This will be the coldest and bravest expression of your commitment to Christ!" the pastor joked.

Everyone laughed.

Full-immersion baptism as an adult means going under, not just sprinkling. It takes on the biblical imagery of death, of going down into the grave and dying to oneself. Overcoming death and rising to new life in Christ, the baptismal candidate comes up out of the water filled with the power of the Spirit, covered by the Blood of the Lamb. She is made new.

And that, quite frankly, was what I wanted: to go down under the water as one person, and come up as someone new. I wanted to be someone who would stand on the edge of the boat in a storm, terrified of the darkness, someone who would dive into the blackness for one lost sheep.

I burst up out of the waters shivering. The white baptismal gown clung to me. I had water in my ears. I stumbled to the shore. In the crowd I saw the faces of people I knew, smiling and clapping, someone running with towels. I saw Jimmy there beside our parents, at the back of the crowd, biting his lip the way he did. He stood in the lineup of people who greeted me. When he hugged me, it was one-armed and distant.

"Hey, way to go," he said, but his voice was flat. "Congratulations."

I wanted to say, Jim, it's me.

But I knew it wouldn't make any difference. It seemed I had officially joined up, marched off to a sunny, Sunday world without him.

"There you are!" said the woman who'd confessed earlier that week that she had been praying faithfully for me for two years. I could see she felt as if she'd succeeded. I was a project that was now completed; her prayers for me had been answered in this step of baptism. She hugged me tightly and sang a few bars of a hymn for me on this special occasion. "I am washed, yes I'm washed, I am washed in the blood, I'm all washed in the blood of the lamb," she sang to me, holding back tears, smiling into my eyes. "Heather, you are washed in the blood of the lamb."

I just smiled and nodded. What else could I say?

The festivities had begun; people passed cards and a few small presents. I watched Jimmy turn and wander off, disappearing up the trail to the large wooden chapel. It was the chapel we'd gone to at Teen Camp, when neither of us knew how dark the days ahead would be.

That year Jimmy hadn't wanted to go to Bible camp at all, but I'd been counting the days. I was eleven and eager. We were in different age groups, so I almost never saw him except for catching a glimpse of him across the room in the swarm of kids at dinner. There were water fights and banana split parties and games of Capture the Flag in the dark. And there were cabin discussions led by kind volunteers who genuinely cared.

On the last day of chapel, every camper had gathered for the final service, just before we went to pack our things to go home. The speaker asked us all to close our eyes and bow our heads.

"If you've been at camp this week and you've felt God calling you, I want to invite you to come forward."

These are important moments for camp directors. The numbers need to be up there. I'm not suggesting there was any insincerity that day, but the stage is generally set for "the call" at the end to have maximum impact. When you're a camper, you're not aware of any of this.

Everyone was silent, stopped wiggling, closed their eyes tightly.

The speaker had gentle words, asking all those who had never asked Jesus to be their Lord and Savior to come to pray with the team at the front.

"We'll wait for you," he said. "I know there are people God is calling right now. Even if you're at the back, you just come forward; don't worry about anyone around you."

And even though I knew we were meant to keep our eyes closed tightly, I couldn't help but peek through just a crack in my eyelids to see what was happening.

When I did, I couldn't believe what I saw.

There was Jimmy, coming down the aisle from the very back of the room, on the other side of the chapel, not just walking but running. I opened my eyes wide, stunned, unable to stop watching. The man at the front put his arm around Jimmy's shoulder and gave him a strong, welcoming squeeze. I couldn't see his face, but I saw him rest against the man at the front.

Afterward, I tried to look for him, but with the kids laughing and exchanging phone numbers, the staff calling out good-byes, promising to see us all next year, I was swept along, and I couldn't see him anywhere.

Jimmy never mentioned it, and I never let on that I knew.

Ten years had passed since that day I'd seen him running down the aisle of the chapel. I changed out of the dripping white baptismal gown, quickly dried my hair, and put on the dress I'd bought for the reception, floral with a wide belt that made my waist look thin. I stared at myself in the mirror. I felt ridiculous.

We enjoyed a luncheon with trays of tuna salad and egg salad sandwiches, cakes and cookies and pickles. There were photos taken of families with pretty bouquets of flowers.

Then we went back to our ordinary lives, just the same. Deeply, sadly, regrettably the same.

16

By November of 1989, five months had passed since my baptism at Ness Lake. One Sunday evening, after the evening service, the young adults group hung over the backs of the pews, chatting, deciding which restaurant to go to for dessert and coffee. The girls flirted with the boys, home from Bible school or university looking to find a wife. The girls were waiting to be claimed by the boys they'd loved their whole lives.

A new restaurant had just opened on the safe end of George Street. No one in the group had been there yet and someone had a coupon for a free dessert.

"I don't think we should go down there," a girl said. "I hate seeing all those people and it smells so bad down there."

George Street was just a short street on the edge of downtown, maybe three blocks with any action to speak of, a couple of old hotels with rundown bars, and one traffic light. But it was a street that made people afraid.

George Street was the place that collected the people whose lives had been ravaged, torn to pieces, and thrown away, like pages ripped from a book. The shreds blew down the lanes and ended up under benches, on heat vents in the cold, or swept into a corner outside the Holiday Inn. Collectively, the city noticed them as a problem, but individually they were nothing.

The town's second movie theatre was on George Street. Once, after the movies and before I was old enough to understand a place like George Street, our car was stopped at a red light. I noticed a girl at the corner. She had a very short skirt and her legs looked cold, but she was dressed in white tassels and beads that shimmered on her dark skin. She was beautiful. Her long black hair fell across her face like silk and when she brushed it from her eyes with her hand, a white feather from her earring fell out and floated to the ground.

"That girl," I said pointing. "She lost her beautiful earring."

"She's not beautiful," my mother said. "You shouldn't be looking at her."

I stared at the back of my mother's seat.

She *was* beautiful.

A car pulled up across the street from her and rolled down the window. The driver whistled. She laughed and walked across the street in her white high heels, tall and dangerous, her tassels swinging at her thighs. She slid into the car. The feather blew down the street and disappeared. Years later, when I heard, for the first time, the story of the woman who wiped the feet of Jesus with her hair, I could see her long silky hair in my mind.

When the traffic light finally changed, I caught sight of a man sleeping under a coat on the sidewalk, not quite on George Street but nearby. Then a native woman staggered out onto the street and slammed her fist on the hood of a car; people started to yell. We drove away. In those days, George Street would never have made me think of my brother who was, at that moment, sitting quietly, buckled in the seatbelt right beside me.

George Street stayed in mind much longer than my parents knew. When I was old enough to take the bus by myself, I sometimes went to the edge of George Street, just to see what it was like in the day. There were no lepers on George Street, but it was the place I believed, even then, that God would care about. He'd have been there, sitting at a long table in a café, sorting through the shreds of paper he'd found on some heat vent, piecing them together like a jigsaw puzzle, reassembling the pages of someone's damaged life, smoothing them out as best he could, never once getting smoke in his eyes.

The dessert group decided to try the new George Street restaurant on the condition that one of the boys drove the girls. They climbed into the backseat of his car, giggling.

I drove my own car. When I stopped to put money in the parking meter, absentmindedly because none was needed at night, an old man with a bushy yellowing beard stepped out from an alleyway; I nearly walked into him.

"Oh!" I said, startled. "Sorry."

"No, I'm sorry," he said, covering his mouth with his hand, backing away.

He smelled of alcohol and damp, soiled clothes. There was something in his eyes that I was compelled to look at. I could not pull my gaze away. It was shininess—the same shininess that I had begun to see in Jim's eyes almost every time I saw him. The more he drank, the more he tried to blink it away, smiling awkwardly. The man on the street had the same shine.

It was not a shine that came from inside of him, not from an inner light, not some sunny day occurring in his heart. No, the shininess in his eyes was a hunger that attracted the light nearby, reflecting off a cold surface, like the glint off a vodka bottle lying in a ditch.

"Have you got any change you could spare?" the man said.

Clearly I did, I had the coins for the meter in my hand, so I gave them to him.

"God bless you, miss." He turned and stepped back into the alley.

"You too," I said and hurried to catch up to the others who were waiting across the street for me.

"You shouldn't give those people money," someone said, giving me a little advice. "They'll only buy drugs with it. It makes the problem worse."

"Those people don't need money, they need the Lord," someone said.

Everyone in the dessert group agreed.

As we ate dessert, I was lost in my own thoughts. I wondered about that man on the street with the yellowing beard, if he'd had a sister who'd tried to help him and failed. I wondered if he'd been the kind of brother who could catch fireflies.

"Are you okay?" someone said.

"Yeah, I'm fine. Just tired."

We walked back to our cars together, the two girls shuffling their feet along the slippery sidewalk. The man with the yellowing beard was nowhere to be seen, but at the corner, leaning up against a wall, stood a woman who seemed to be about my age. My parents would have called her a "lady of the night," but she was more of a girl. She had thick black eyeliner and silver eye shadow up to her brows. She wore bright red lipstick, tight jeans, and thigh-high black leather boots. Her fur-collared coat must have been a thrift-store find.

A thin ribbon of smoke from her right hand drifted up her arm. I knew the sensation of the smoke sliding up the wrist from the palm of your hand, warmth on a chilly night. I wondered if she, too, had stolen cigarettes from her father's pack when she was twelve.

We stood in conspicuous silence at the corner, waiting for the light to change. When we started across the street, someone in the group jeered in a whisper not meant for her to hear, "Hey, I thought Halloween was last month."

When everyone broke out in a nervous kind of laughter, I glanced back to see if she'd heard. When she saw me look back, she stuck her middle finger up. I thought about running back, lying to her, saying the joke was not about her, but I didn't.

"Hey, she just fingered us!" someone said.

Yes, I thought—*us.*

She fingered *us*; such a little word, but it made me see myself right there on the street, the lights of George Street in the background, me there in the midst of the giggling dessert group. I belonged in the dessert group as I'd never belonged before; I'd never felt more ashamed.

The shine from the eyes of the man on George Street stayed with me for days.

"I don't know why I can't stop thinking about it," I said over lunch in the college cafeteria. I was sitting with my friend, Maureen, sharing an order of large fries and gravy. Christmas carols played in the background over the lunch hour—an attempt to bring a little cheer to the drab surroundings.

Maureen didn't know the details of the night, but I'd told her what I could about it. She wasn't a churchgoer in those days. I couldn't explain the shame I'd felt that night, or how my brain had been flooded with images of me just standing there in the circle of people—the "people of God"—scorning the world on George Street.

It wasn't just that man. It was Jimmy.

It was the thought of him digging in garbage cans, begging for quarters on the edge of some town he'd disappeared to, made all the worse by the Christmas carols on the radio, the shoppers bustling, the families gathering. It was the thought of Jimmy as an old man, alone in a run-down hotel room at Christmas.

And it wasn't just Jimmy. It was the Church.

I believed in the Church. Not the church I attended, so much, but I believed in the *idea* of the Church. I believe in it, still. The Church should be a place that glows with lanterns lit by fireflies to be carried to the corners of the night. And because I believed in it but I didn't see it, I couldn't let it go.

I must *do* something, I thought. But what could I do?

I am tempted to distance my adult self from the young self I was then, but I won't do that. I wonder why this is still important to me? Instead, I will honor her trying, even if trying was not enough. I don't excuse myself here, but I didn't know what I know now. Enthusiasm is not enough; when we step into the night without a lantern, sometimes we get lost along the way.

It was 1989. It was the year that powerless people had risen up all over the world. It was the year that Nadia Comaneci fled Romania; the year that students protested in Tiananmen Square; the world gasped at images of a little man with shopping bags standing up to the tanks on the street, daring them to take him on. It was the year of the Berlin Wall coming down, people weeping with joy as they threw their bodies behind sledge-hammers beating against the wall that had imprisoned them.

Small people with hammers were changing the world, making things new. The Church could be different—*should* be different—I knew. Perhaps all it needed was a nudge. I was twenty-one and full of hope;

surely, I was capable of a nudge. So, as if I could throw a line from my world to the world of the yellow-bearded man on George Street, fastening a rope between us, between the man with the shiny eyes and me, between George Street and the Church, between the sun and the moon, I decided to invite him to church—to the Christmas Carol Service.

As absurd as it sounds, somehow I had confused them, the Church and God, as if they were the same, as if delivering someone to the steps of the church was the same as bringing him to God. In truth, my intentions were rooted in kindness. I wanted him not to be alone, or cold or hungry this Christmas; there would be carols, children laughing, and people to be with. I let myself imagine it. It was something I could *do*.

That night I decided to make up an invitation to the Carol Service. I hoped I could find him. I bought a package of gold foil-lined envelopes because I'd wanted it to feel dignified.

The next day Maureen arrived at college with a trunk full of dishes and pots and pans and small household items.

"You can't just invite him to church," she'd said. "You should probably help him get back on his feet." My generous, spirited, amazing friend. Why had I only thought of getting him to church? She'd emptied her hope chest of the things she'd been saving for years and packed them into the trunk of her car.

"I don't seem to need these things at the moment, but it sounds like he does."

Maureen and I drove off in her car in search of the man I hoped we'd be able to find, me clutching the gold foil envelope, her driving the trunk full of precious things to a man she'd never met, both of us carrying what mattered most. We were young and filled with faith and optimism that afternoon, the sun was shining and the world was covered in fresh fallen snow.

We found him sitting on a bench near the Holiday Inn on George Street. It seemed that even finding him had been a miracle. I didn't know then that the people on the streets of Prince George were a community of people who belonged to one another and would have been found by

anyone who bothered to look long enough. But that afternoon it seemed
to be the miraculous proof we needed, a sign we were doing the right
thing.

He had the same shiny eyes as I'd remembered from weeks before.
It was a strange feeling. He looked at me blankly of course, not knowing me from any of the dozens of people who passed by each day. But
I'd carried him in my mind for days, and felt like I knew him in some
distant way.

"Hi," I said, smiling and introducing myself, trying hard not to
sound like I was selling something. "I know this might sound unusual,
but I've seen you before and you've been on my mind." I explained about
the Carol Service and then added, "I brought you this invitation and was
wondering if you'd like to come as my guest."

He blinked his eyes a few times, trying to take it all in, and then
reached for the invitation, holding it in his hand and not opening it.

"I didn't know your name," I said, apologetically pointing to the
envelope. "Otherwise I'd have written it on the invitation." I could see
him looking me over then, taking his time, thinking carefully.

"Bruce," he said. "My name is Bruce." He handed it back to me
before he opened it and then began to spell it, motioning for me to make
the necessary change. "B-R-U-C-E." I fumbled in my purse for a pen
and when I found it, I wrote his name in careful letters across the front
of the invitation.

"Thank you very much," he said, reaching for the invitation and
opening it slowly, being careful not to tear it.

"You're welcome," I said and stood waiting for him to respond.

"Thank you," he said again nodding, staring down at the paper in his
hand. "When did you say it was?" He closed the invitation and slipped it
back in the envelope. He couldn't read.

"It's next week, Wednesday at 7:30. If you'd like to come, I could
pick you up." He nodded and stared down at the ground.

"Been a long time since I been to church. When I was a boy, sure,
and when we first got married—not since."

Both Maureen and I were quiet, not sure what to do next.

"Would you like to come?" I said carefully.

"Yes," he said matter-of-factly. "I'd like that."

When we told him that Maureen had brought some things for him to use if he needed them, just to help him get back on his feet, he agreed to take them. Bruce lived in one room in an old hotel. His room was not locked and was only a couple of blocks away. He said he didn't have any church clothes to speak of, and I told him it didn't matter. We managed to fill his empty shelves with the things Maureen had found for him and a couple of bags of groceries. We said good-bye, and I told him I'd pick him up. We agreed to meet at the bench; I knew there was a good chance he might not even remember.

At 6:55 p.m. that evening, I pulled up across the street from the bench, and he was there waiting. He had his hair slicked back with some kind of lotion and the same stained coat and pants, but he had a shirt on underneath that I could tell was once white. He smelled more of Aqua Velva than of alcohol.

"Bruce!" I called out to him from across the street, pulling my coat shut and sliding my shoes on the ice to cross the street to greet him. He stood up and turned to me and smiled a large, relieved smile that exposed his missing teeth.

"Merry Christmas!" I said to him and handed him some baking I'd wrapped with a ribbon. He stared down at the baking and touched the red bow with his stained fingers. His hand trembled. He said nothing, just nodded, staring down at the ribbon.

Because the road was slippery and he seemed frail, we linked arms and shuffled carefully across the street. When we got in the car he could not manage the seatbelt and I could see it had been a long time since he'd been in a car. I reached over and helped him buckle it up.

We had a short drive to the church, but on the way I learned he had a daughter somewhere in Alberta and he'd once had a wife. He hadn't heard from either of them for twenty or thirty years; he couldn't remember exactly how long. Things had gone wrong for him many years ago, really wrong. That was all he wanted me to know. That was enough. There was a dignity about him then, in the control he had over what he shared with me and what he chose to keep to himself.

On that short drive it began inside of me, a small awareness of myself, some hint that something might not be right with this. The drive took only ten minutes, but in my mind a souring of the evening ahead grew stronger by the second. He had stopped being the man with the shiny eyes and had become Bruce. I felt a warmth between us on that drive, not because I was rescuing him, but because it seemed like we could, for a few moments, be friends.

By the time I got to the church, I had almost changed my mind. Was I doing the right thing? There didn't seem to be a way out any way I looked at it.

We parked at the side entrance instead, purposely now avoiding the main doors. I hoped to slip in the back inconspicuously and get seated just before the opening hymn. When I held the door open for him and he stepped through, I knew, at that moment, it would all be wrong.

There were greeters with corsages posted at every entrance. Betty and John Collins stood like a barricade between the sanctuary and us. They eyed him up and down and smiled quizzically, then sideways at me, and reached for his hand to shake it. John did not just shake his hand, but held it, not squeezing but firmly, for much too long, stubborn and insistent, asking questions, smiling but frowning all at once.

"Visiting with us tonight?" they asked him, eyebrows raised.

"Yes," he said. "Yes, I am." I could see him pull his hand back a little, but John held on tight.

"Well, nice to see you. Are you from town?"

"Yes, yes, I am," said Bruce, glancing sideways at me.

John held his hand firmly, smiling. "What's your name, young fellow?" he said, ribbing him a little. He spoke down to Bruce, the way one would speak to a street person, not a friend invited to the Christmas service.

"This is Bruce," I said quickly stepping in between them, wanting John to let go of his hand, wanting Bruce to feel safe again. I felt the air stiffen around me.

"We're just slipping in the back, excuse us," I said and motioned for him to go ahead while I held the greeters back.

"Welcome, Bruce," John said, repeating his name, letting go of his hand.

Bruce did not answer. At that moment I felt a twinge of guilt, betrayal for something I would not understand until later. I had taken his name, the one thing that belonged to him, the name he had cautiously given me to write respectfully on the invitation, and had given it to strangers he did not trust, strangers who looked at him with contempt.

Then a woman I knew well, a woman I loved and respected, caught my eye and frowned, shaking her head in tiny movements so that only I would notice. Clearly she did not want to embarrass the dirty man with me, but what on earth had I been thinking? It seemed that Bruce and I had become the focal point for whispering. A mother made her children move away from the seats behind us. I had not expected this.

I tried to make conversation with him while we waited for the service to start. Bruce did not respond. Sitting beside him in the church I could smell the street on his clothes. I could not force myself to smell the Aqua Velva. I looked around the room at the sparkly Christmas tree, the pretty Christmas dresses and families going home to extravagant parties and family gatherings.

"I'm sorry," I said to him, finally. There was nothing else I could say. He didn't answer.

It did not occur to me until later, that I'd been fighting some kind of private war with the Church. And Bruce was not only caught in the crossfire, he'd become the artillery. I hadn't meant for it to be like this. There was nowhere for Bruce in the church, no way for him to belong that night, and I was responsible.

I didn't understand it that night. But I felt it. *Forgive me*, I wanted to say to him, but I didn't understand what I'd done. How could I explain *that*? I didn't dare ask him now for something more, first for the gift of his trust and now his forgiveness too.

At the end of the evening Pastor Bill announced that there would be coffee and goodies downstairs for those who could stay. Bruce did not wait for me to ask him.

"I'd like to go home," he said.

"Sure," I said. We didn't talk on the drive through town. I turned on the radio instead.

In the middle of January, I stopped by Bruce's room to say hello. When I knocked, the door pushed open and no one was there, the shelves were empty and there was nothing left of the things Maureen had given him. On the way out I saw him on the street by my car. Did he recognize me? He didn't let on. I could only smell booze when I said hello.

He slurred, when he asked me for money.

I should have emptied my wallet, I should have fallen on the sidewalk at his feet and confessed it all. I should have stripped right down, given him the clothes off my back, weeping.

Instead I told him I didn't have any money and turned to get in my car. I don't know why.

"Take care, Bruce," I said.

He turned and stumbled into the hotel.

17

If it's true that every molecule of water is somehow connected, part of one great sea that flows across the face of the earth, suspended in ice and pools and clouds on its journey across the planet, when these life-giving waters come, it is the sea itself that rises up.

When my brother returned from a trip to Kenya with a photography group, he came back strong and tanned and sober; he came back with beautiful stories that would find their way to the canvas that year. Above my bed hangs the painting of the Serengeti Plains in bloom. Of all the paintings he did when he returned, the Serengeti Plains holds the most meaning for me.

"It was incredible," he'd said. "The rains came one day and by the next morning that dry hill and everything around it for as far as you could see was suddenly green." The incredible life-giving force of water comes like a wave from the sky, releasing the tenacious green that's waiting, just under the surface of the dry earth, to push through.

And so it is with baptism. When you are truly baptized, it is this sea that takes you. It has been waiting. There is nothing you can do, really, but let go, settle in to the strength of the current. There is nothing to be gained by swimming against it. You are called.

And every day, all across the world, on the edge of every beach, the moon calls out to the sea, twice each day. The sea reaches back, answering the moon, leaving its mark, high tide and low, the wet footprint of the great ocean that embraces the planet, the moon singing out in a voice that only the sea can hear.

February was bringing that sea, my third and final baptism, the only baptism that I see, now, as real. It was bringing a watershed moment in my life; I would find myself taken.

I had not forgotten the Carol Service by February, not even with the melting sidewalks of an early spring.

"It was nice of you to bring that man to church at Christmas," a woman from Bible study said to me. She was smiling when she said it, but there was something in her voice.

"Do you know about the Christian Life Centre?" she asked, implying that I should. "It's a place where the down-and-outs can go to church; it might not be so awkward then, you know, for everyone."

I turned and walked to my car. I didn't look back at her. On my way home I stopped at the gas station and bought cigarettes. I chain-smoked half a dozen sitting on a bench thinking, staring up at the moon in the night sky.

I had driven past the building many times before and seen the sign for the *Christian Life Centre* above the tattoo shop. I didn't know it was a place for people who did not belong in ordinary churches. It was on the upper floor in a tired-looking building, a block or two back from George Street. In spite of that disingenuous woman from Bible study, I was curious.

At first I'd parked across the street and just watched people shuffle down the sidewalk, then turn and go through the wrought iron gate and up the narrow staircase. They seemed to disappear into the dark. From the street you could hear the plunking of the piano, the hum of baritone voices reaching for the words of Amazing Grace, singing them like a promise:

I once was lost, but now am found, was blind but now I see.

I met Carol that first night, within moments of stepping inside. She was the caretaker; she lived in the apartment at the back of the Life Centre. Carol helped out with the regular Saturday night service for people who lived downtown, mostly homeless people and people in recovery, people from George Street—the down-and-outs.

The sermons were short and simple, delivered by a strong-looking barrel-chested man who led an AA group at one of the churches. He'd found the Lord and had given his life to ministry and to his tiny wisp of a wife with a grey, frowning face. She was the one plunking out the songs on the piano.

Carol, who had lived on the street for eighteen years, now looked after the place and shepherded lost souls to the Lord through the Life Centre. She'd made herself a new life there. Her old life still showed through in the deep lines around her eyes, the homemade tattoos on her arms, the yellow stains on her fingers.

Once I'd gotten to know her, I felt I could trust her with the questions I had about my brother, as I'd not trusted anyone. Why was that?

"Demons?" she said without looking up. "Of course I believe in demons. Don't you?"

We were getting the sandwiches ready for the service. I listened to the blade of the knife pressing into the cutting board, making a gentle tap each time Carol pressed it through the soft white bread and egg salad tucked inside.

"I don't know," I said.

"What's not to believe?" She kept cutting the sandwiches into quarters and arranging them on the plate. "Can you grab the napkins? They're in the bottom drawer." My question didn't startle her. It was as if I'd said the most ordinary thing.

Carol wore a large curly wig to cover her brittle, thinning hair, the fallout from years of hard living.

"If you'd seen some of the things I've seen you wouldn't be asking—you'd just know," she said, shaking her head, remembering. Her cigarette had gone out in the ashtray. "You ask any one of these people here tonight about demons and they'll tell you."

There was an edge to her voice. Was she annoyed or disappointed I was asking? It was hard to tell.

"I'm not asking because I don't believe," I explained. "I'm asking because I just don't know what to think anymore."

She turned to look up at me, waiting for me to go on, reached for the lighter and flicked it to light her cigarette. Her cheeks seemed to collapse into bony caves when she took a deep drag.

Finally I said it. "Actually I'm asking because I think my brother might have a demon or something." There. It was out.

"Well if he does, he needs the Lord. And even then, he needs all the help he can get. Trust me, I know."

She started to rearrange the sandwiches in a fan on the plate, adjusting them so the crusts were lined up. At the time I didn't pay attention to this, only now, when I replay it in my mind, I notice that's what she's doing. She was making the plate for the evening service beautiful. Did her mother teach her to do this? Did her mother make egg sandwiches like this, arranging them artistically on a glass plate in a sunny kitchen, before her daughter left home to live on the street, before her arms were tattooed and marked up by the world?

"If he has a demon, he needs deliverance," she said.

We stopped the conversation when someone else arrived.

I noticed Charlie the very first Saturday night at the Christian Life Centre. He hid his face behind a mop of shiny black hair that swung thickly over his eyes and a hand that was missing two fingers. I only saw his full face once. He was in his twenties and had left the Indian Reserve in Burns Lake a few years before. The other thing about Charlie was his bright blue ski jacket, turquoise like the sky.

At the Christian Life Centre—or anywhere on George Street for that matter—the turquoise jacket stood out. The winter brought out dark heavy coats or grey blankets with shapes hunched inside for warmth, bodies breathing and slouching on benches or tucked beneath vents. Even in the summer, people who lived in the First Avenue hotel rooms wore clothes stained to brown and grey by their lives. The world of people on George Street seemed unable to hold any color.

So Charlie's new turquoise jacket was the talk of the Saturday evening service at the Life Centre when he first arrived with it; he'd been up north at his uncle's funeral. The coat had belonged to his uncle.

"Pretty fancy new coat you got there, Charlie," Carol teased.

Charlie laughed quietly but didn't look up. He didn't speak. He had a severe cleft palate that he kept hidden behind the hair that hung across his face like a heavy curtain. Charlie didn't stay long on Saturday evenings. He waited until the sandwiches and cookies were served, politely had a cup of coffee alone on a chair in the corner, and then carefully filled his pockets with food to take with him. I was careful to keep my distance. It seemed to suit him. But once, when I was searching silently for the sugar cubes in the drawers, he reached into a cupboard and pulled out a new box for me.

"Thanks," I said. He nodded behind his hair. Even if he was silent, he noticed everything that happened around him.

"He's a good kid," Carol said. "He just gets himself into trouble sometimes."

When I went to the Life Centre on Saturday nights, I went alone. I didn't talk about it to anyone. It belonged in a private part of my life, but by then most of my life had become private. Even the relationships I'd had seemed to belong to someone else's life.

I dressed in jeans and a grey sweatshirt on Saturday nights. I could almost disappear in grey. And that was what I wanted more than anything else: to be invisible. I wanted to observe the Saturday night shuffle of people who needed a warm place to stop, a few songs, a cup of coffee, and food to go home with. I wanted to understand.

Slipping along the Continental Divide of the Canadian Rockies is a short little stream without much water to speak of. It's called Divide Creek, but it's more than a creek. Somewhere up there, in the middle of the gurgling waters of Divide Creek, is the gentle invisible edge of one of the continent's greatest watersheds, where gravitational forces on each side push and pull in opposite directions. What happens in the current of that creek changes everything for a little leaf or twig floating along the surface, skipping along the top of the Canadian Rockies for a short distance—the living water of the earth rushing, flowing, consecrating, taking.

Suddenly, the creek forks, separating into two long, water highways that lead thousands of miles in opposite directions. One stream finds its way north, emptying into the Hudson Bay, the other joins the Kicking Horse River and winds up in the Pacific Ocean, thousands of miles apart. Some small critical moment determines everything for a leaf being carried in the current, nudged a little left or right just before the fork.

This is a watershed moment. Nothing will be the same for the leaf. The world is fundamentally altered by what happens in that one small moment, by what these waters do to that leaf.

This is baptism.

On a Sunday morning in February, I was on my way to the morning service at the Evangelical Free Church dressed in a skirt and a white blouse.

I pulled up to the building and saw all the cars in the parking lot, just the same as every week before, every week for four years, the same families, the same ideas, the same jokes, the same ordinary emptiness. Something in me just could not do it. I could not go in that morning. I decided to keep driving, with nowhere else to go really, just not there.

There was fresh snow, and I liked being the first car making tracks. I drove downtown just to drive, just to have a reason not to go to church. It was a Sunday morning, so the streets would be empty. I thought about stopping somewhere for coffee and found myself driving slowly past the Christian Life Centre.

In the alley beside the tattoo shop was a bright turquoise lump lying in the snow, it was turquoise like the sky, turquoise like Charlie's jacket.

I stopped the car and jumped out, slipping quickly across the street in my heels.

It was not just a lump, it was a body in the snow. The body wasn't moving. It was Charlie's jacket, cut open with white stuffing escaping from the slashes.

"Charlie?" I said. "Charlie, is that you?"

"Help me," he said. He turned his face and looked up at me, without his hair to cover his face. He was covered in blood, the snow was red beneath him.

"They cut my fucking jacket."

This was the watershed, the Divide Creek moment that would alter my life forever.

"Can you get up?" I said.

"I'm fucking bleeding."

There was a lot of blood. Was he dying? I hated myself for being so weak, for standing in the snow trembling. He needed a doctor.

"Stay still," I said. I ran to yell up the stairs of the Life Centre to Carol who I hoped was there. She would know what to do.

"Carol!" I shouted out. "Carol, are you there?" The gate was locked.

No answer.

"Carol!" I screamed.

No answer.

I ran back to Charlie.

"Can you walk?"

"I don't know," he said.

Baptism, typically, happens with water. But some of us are baptized in fresh fallen snow, with the blood of a stranger lying on the street. This baptism happened without an audience or a priest or a pastor. In these few moments, in an alley near George Street, this baptism walked me from death to new life. This is where I died to myself, where I went down into the snow on my knees, where I kneeled on the sidewalk and reached for him trembling, terrified of the blood, terrified of his face.

"Let's do this together," I said. I leaned down and turned him a little. He reached up and put his arms around my neck.

"Okay, let's lift. Just a second." I was thinking of my skirt, for heaven's sake. Why? I hiked it up high so I could kneel in the snow and we got up off the ground somehow. He was a small man so I could carry most of his weight. We fumbled across the street to my car and I managed to kick open the door and slide him in.

He needed to lean forward or he would bleed from his stomach, he said. I shut the door and went around to my side and hopped in. What if he died in my car? He slumped forward then and closed his eyes.

"You've got to stay awake, Charlie," I said, because I knew that's what people were supposed to say. The hospital was close but it seemed to take forever to get him there. He was shaking.

"They cut my fucking jacket," he said quietly.

"It's okay, I can sew it!" But the jacket was full of blood; there would be no fixing that.

When we arrived at the hospital emergency entrance, I left him in the car and ran in shouting. They sent two attendants out to help. I stood back and watched.

"You should go and get washed," the nurse said shaking her head, looking at my white blouse stained in blood.

I looked down at my clothes. "Yeah," I said. "I will."

The attendants took Charlie in through the doors and he disappeared.

I drove home slowly, my legs quaking, nearly too weak to use the clutch. Somewhere in my head I heard humming; it was a hymn:

I am washed in the blood, I am washed in the blood, I am washed in the blood of the lamb . . .

In my room, I stripped off my clothes and put them in a garbage bag. I climbed into the shower and let the steam from the hot water fill my lungs. I sat down on the floor of the shower and wept. Everything was wrong: the world was wrong; I was wrong; Charlie's face, pleading and vulnerable; his turquoise jacket cut to shreds; me in my high heels, carrying him to my car; me in my warm shower, about to choose another pair of pastel pants from the stack in my closet. *All of it was wrong.*

I could get cleaned up and drop into the evening service by 6 p.m. and no one would ever know that the universe inside my head had broken in half, as if the cell structures in my body had been rearranged, as if the path that light travelled inside my eyes was altered that afternoon. A kind of frantic state came over me. Perhaps madness. Some might have dismissed it as shock, but I knew better. It was as if the dam that had contained me had been struck with a sledgehammer, destroying the mortar that held the stones in place. The wall was irreparable; the water had begun to flow.

I stared at the hangers of pretty things, the folded sunshine-colored cotton pants, the white blouse with petals embroidered on the collar, pretty, colorful outfits that were no good to a man dying on the street. They were wrong.

Slowly, I began to take down the stacks of things, slipping the skirts and blouses from the hangers until they fell on the floor. I stripped the closet of everything that was pink and yellow and pretty. I took every pair of church shoes and the box of matching earrings; I took the dress I wore to a summer wedding, the sundress with lace around the edge of the sleeves and stuffed everything into two large orange garbage bags. I dragged the bags behind me down the spiral staircase and heaved them to the car.

I didn't know what this had to do with Charlie, but it felt as if there was something right beginning to happen inside of me. I grabbed another bag and went back to my room, I emptied my drawers, I took every ounce of makeup I could find, I took my curling iron and blow dryer and hairspray and shoved them in a bag. What I left in my closet were a few simple things, jeans and t-shirts, my green cloth jacket, my grey sweatshirt.

There was something purifying about this, sacramental perhaps. It was not about the things themselves. It was about who I was inside of them. I got in my car and drove the bags downtown to the steps of the Salvation Army store. There was no going back.

Charlie would survive what happened that day, but a part of me would not. I was making myself new. I was a leaf that had slipped into the stream, travelling fast away from the world I'd become part of, far away from the dessert group, the Bible study ladies, the Evangelical Free Church.

I was the current; I was the water; I was the flow. I could feel the sea itself rising up, the moon pulling hard from the sky.

18

$\mathcal{I}$t doesn't help to wonder now if things might have been different for my brother if I'd stayed with him. But I wonder anyway. I didn't intentionally leave him, but I didn't stay. I would go for help. I would find answers. That's what I told us both.

I didn't know then that 10 percent of the world's population hears voices. I didn't know that articulate and resilient people would come out the other side and begin to talk about their voices, coming to an understanding of them as a part of themselves; that these voices often expressed a deeply damaged emotional world that could not otherwise be expressed.

I didn't know that the medical professionals who sought to help my brother did not, themselves, understand. I believed in the authority of the doctors in the way I believed in the Church. Both the medical world and Church leaders found their identity in being the ones with the answers, the ones with authority.

None of them were about to let on that they were guessing.

I don't blame them, exactly; I needed them to have the answers as much as they needed to be the ones who had them. I needed them to take authority; I gave it to them, willingly. Because if they didn't have the answers, who did?

Jim was careful about who he trusted after our family doctor told him he was a drunk, that's all there was to it. There was nothing wrong with him; he needed to kick the booze. Period. Psychiatrists and their teams did assessments and decided he was quite normal, maybe a little depressed, but generally fine.

Jimmy did not, of course, let on. If he made mention of the voices at all to other people, it was in passing, as a joke perhaps, gauging reactions to see if they understood. He would not be ridiculed.

He understood—by then, we both understood—the voices were demons: Jimmy, because it was what he experienced, and me, because I wanted not to doubt him. And with both of us operating from a kind of biblical paradigm, the matter grew more and more complex. How difficult it is to see clearly when our understanding of the world is shaped by belief systems that are flawed. The voices must be demons. What else could they be? Thank God the world talks now; we know more.

It was clear to me then that Jimmy was worried about my safety and about what the demons would do to me. I was too.

I heard a TED talk recently, given by an articulate young woman who survived an experience like my brother's and is now healthy and functioning well. She remembers sitting outside her parents' bedroom door at night with a knife, protecting them from the voices. What could her parents have thought when they saw her there?

I know what I thought.

What was he doing out there, lurking in the night by my door?

I didn't want to know; I was afraid.

If I'd known then what I know now, would I have chosen to leave him?

But perhaps we don't really choose the course of our lives. Maybe the earth holds the markings for our lives already, whether or not we are aware. When water escapes from a hole in the dam to find itself hanging in the sky, suspended in midair for that partial moment before it hits dry ground, the grooves in the forest, the stones and stumps, the contours of the land, already know the path it will take. They're not surprised. The streambed is there long before the water finds it. It's nonsense to think that the water will choose its way.

It happened almost by accident. I'd first heard about Regent College from friends of a friend. They spoke highly of it. But everyone agreed: people often go to Regent for answers and leave with more questions. This intrigued me, but I hadn't paid much attention to Regent College, at least not in a serious way.

Not until I found the book.

The final church I visited was the First Baptist. The minister had double booked, mixed up his schedule, so I sat in the chair outside the secretary's office waiting for him to arrive. Beside the chair was a box of books, good-quality secondhand books on a range of topics, presumably left for the church library.

The book on the top caught my eye. It was a book called *I Believe in Satan's Downfall*.[1] I stared at the cover for a while and then made my decision. I tried to be as inconspicuous as I could, then I shoved the book in my purse when no one was looking. I said good-bye to the secretary, promising her I'd call again and promising myself I'd return the book sometime. I never did.

I read the pages carefully and then rushed to show the key parts to Jimmy:

> *If a demon inhabits a person, it can only show itself through that person's personality, through his psychological or physical expression. Therefore it is all too easy to mistake demonic for other manifestations of the body and mind. The following is only a rough guide, gleaned largely from experience. It makes no claim to be exhaustive.*

The book's author was Reverend Canon Dr. Michael Green, a professor at Regent College, "one of the world's leading evangelists, renowned

---

1. London: Hodder & Stoughton Limited, 1988.

amongst evangelicals worldwide." This meant he had credibility, and that mattered to me.

I didn't know then that he was principal of St. John's College in Nottingham, that he was rector of St. Aldate's Church, Oxford, or that he was advisor to the archbishops of Canterbury and York. I paid little attention to the Scripture verses quoted and the historical developments he traced. When I first read it, I was impatient for answers, flipping for something tangible, scanning pages, my eyes racing across his words:

> One of the gifts of the Holy Spirit is called "discernment of spirits" (1 Cor. 12:10) and it refers to this very question of discerning whether or not a person is demonized. Hebrews 5:14 points to the same thing and indicates that discerning good from evil is something which grows in the mature Christian. I find that, quite unsought by me, I possess this gift, and it is very useful.

This was a man with answers.
He continued:

> I have never yet known it to be wrong, though it does not always operate when the demons are not manifesting themselves. It is a certain physical sensation. I felt it first in Ghana when somebody fainted right across from me at the moment of commitment to Christ: a feeling of unutterable evil led me simply to call on the name of Jesus again and again.

Every time I read this sentence, I knew what he meant, the feeling, deep inside where the shivery edge of the soul trembles quietly, careful not to let the fear shout out, careful to stand tall and courageous, as if there was no way to be afraid. I knew the feeling in the room, the stillness of the air. I knew it before my brother spoke, this physical reaction I'd felt surging like electrical currents. I knew the look in his eyes, the way sometimes, on nights alone, he'd turn his head and I felt the air tighten. This much, I understood.

> The most sensational, and one of the earliest experiences I had when I was entering a room where a possessed person was standing (and raving). The person screeched aloud and shrank to the wall at the arrival of another Christian. I felt an immediate, almost palpable, sense of evil,

went up to the person and commanded the evil thing that was causing the trouble to name itself. This it did, to my great surprise. Then having nothing but the gospels to go on, I commanded it by its name to come out. It did—and the person crashed to the ground!

By the time I finished this sentence again, I knew I had to find this man.

I would go to Regent College.

19

Regent College is a graduate school for Christian Studies at the University of British Columbia. It is not on East Hastings Street, and yet I often found myself there at night and not at Regent. East Hastings Street in Vancouver is a place busy with addicts and homeless people, prostitutes and dealers, the elderly who carry mice in their pockets for company. In one afternoon you can count dozens of people talking to the air, cursing the voices and demons that follow them. It's nothing like George Street; George Street is Disneyland compared to East Vancouver.

I often spent the evening hours alone, riding buses across the city to nowhere. Was this my own kind of sackcloth and ashes, a kind of repentance for having walked away?

Sometimes I thought about Bruce and Charlie, about Carol and the Life Centre, but mostly I thought about Jimmy. He'd married Uta a few weeks before I'd left for Regent in September.

"You wanna know something?" he'd said to me the night before the wedding. "I don't even want to get married."

"What?" I said. "What are you talking about?"

But I listened.

"Jim, it's just wedding jitters, people feel that way all the time." But even as the words came out of my mouth, I knew it wasn't true. I could see he didn't want this.

"Well, it's not too late," I said, knowing that for him it probably was.

"Oh yes, it is," he said. "Nothing I can do about it now."

He was right. He would be unable to do anything about it. To cancel a wedding and walk out on the bride would take a person with tremendous personal strength. That wasn't Jimmy. He couldn't ask the bank attendant for new checks because he was afraid of being embarrassed.

How could he ever stand up to the darkness that had taken hold inside of him?

Riding the busses was meditational, even prayerful. But whether or not it helped me understand my brother, I'm not sure. There I was, doing the only thing I knew how to do: riding the bus and thinking. But the comforting thing about riding busses is that mostly everyone on a bus is alone. On a bus you are just like everyone else. I was working at accepting this, that my life would be a solitary one, the glass walls around me grew thicker with the growing complexity of my brother; it would be impossible for someone else to understand.

Once my brother came to visit, but he stayed with Lance. Lance was like a brother to us both; he was Jimmy's best friend. He'd been the kind of kid in school who'd played the piano and carried a briefcase; he was the kind of loyal friend you could count on, no matter what, no matter how bad things got.

Lance could outplay Billy Joel himself, we used to say as he hammered the keys and stomped the peddles, thumping out every Billy Joel song ever written, friends and family gathered around the piano on a Saturday night.

"Sing us a song you're the Piano Man . . . Sing us a song tonight!" we hollered, recklessly off-key but living the song right there in that moment. "One more, one more!" the parents would call out from their stools perched around the room. Lance always had one more for us.

While I was at Regent, I lived in a Mennonite residence with no room for guests. So when Jimmy came to Vancouver, Lance was there for him. Jimmy hadn't really come to visit; he came to escape. He was leaving his wife, moving back home probably, he wasn't sure; he was in Vancouver to leave it all behind for a while. His eyes were shiny.

When I sat beside him on the bus, I could hardly breathe. He stunk of booze, the way empty bottles smell soured and filthy after the party's over, alcohol seeping through his pores, filling the whole bus. He walked hanging on to things, talking loudly, making jokes that only drunk people would laugh at. The lady in front us moved to another seat. I could not force myself to be close to him. There was something so vulnerable about him, I couldn't bear it. I could not be present with him, not like this. He had come undone so completely, I could hardly look at him. After a few hours I lied to him, told him I had to go, I had a class I'd forgotten about.

I called Lance. He agreed to pick him up. When he pulled up in his car, I felt the way I did that day when I'd run over a small dog when I first learned to drive; I couldn't bear it, I was just relieved that someone had come. I couldn't be who my brother needed me to be that day, and I couldn't be who that dog had needed me to be. I couldn't wrap my brother in a blanket and hold him close to me, even though it was the very thing he needed. Someone needed to take that broken boy in her arms and hold him, not minding about the blood, not noticing he might not make it. Someone needed to love that boy without wondering what was wrong with him, without fearing that the darkness might never go away, that there mightn't be any answers. Someone needed to sit with him on a bench in the park, to be with him in the most sisterly, loving way, with no longing for the boy that once filled her jar with fireflies and no disappointment for the way things had turned out.

I was not that someone.

I was not nearly enough of what I needed to be.

When they drove away, I got on the bus alone.

The first time I went to Vancouver's Eastside on my own, it was a hot September afternoon. Indian summer, my father would have said. I looked for some green space, the cool of a park. From a distance, it was easy to mistake the bodies on the lawn for sunbathers. But Oppenheimer Park in East Vancouver in 1990 was not a place for sunbathers.

Heroin and crack, bodies strewn across the lawn; people were propped asleep against a fence, in an alley behind a metal bin, upside down on the steps or curled up asleep next to sleeping dogs on the sidewalk. When I saw those dogs curled up beside those bodies, I thought of Prince in the storm and saw the scene over and over again in my mind.

We'd had a black lab once, called Prince. My father brought him home from the vet, rescuing him from being put down by owners who'd had enough. The vet didn't exactly know why the owners wanted the dog put down; he seemed healthy, just had a bit of trouble with thunder.

"He's a nice-looking dog," my dad said. "The vet said he was healthy and strong, just hates thunder apparently."

So we were careful. When we went out, we locked him in the basement, just in case. Every time a storm came, my father stroked the dog's neck and whispered gently near his ear. The dog's skin quivered on top of his muscles even though he was lying still at our feet.

Once, when the skies had been clear for months, a storm blew in unexpectedly, gathering the strength of the entire stormless season. Prince was home without the comfort of our family, locked in the basement. When the storm passed over us, we worried about the dog.

"He's a dog, he's not a person," my father said. So we didn't go home.

But when we arrived at the mudroom door, no dog met us; there was no bouncing and barking. That was when we knew something was wrong.

The dog had dug a hole in the door from the basement that was two feet wide. It's true it wasn't a strong door, not built to hold back that kind of fear. In the family room, the couch cushions had been thrown off the couches and onto the floor; my dad's office chair was knocked over as if a burglar had broken in. We climbed the stairs.

The living room was in disarray, cushions and magazines were scattered everywhere, my mother's African violet stand was smashed and the soil was dumped and spread across the carpet. The tablecloth in the dining room was pulled to the floor, and the salt and pepper shakers had crashed to the ground.

My dad whistled for the dog.

Silence.

"Here boy, come on, you're okay." He whistled again, crouching down, listening.

Where *was* he?

Then we heard him whine from my parents' room.

"Prince, come on boy, you're okay."

The dog slunk out of the bedroom, sliding on his belly, shaking, pleading, scared as hell, my dad said.

"Come here, boy. You'll be okay."

My dad whispered, he didn't scold the dog, which surprised me. Instead he reached for the dog's collar and took hold of it firmly, then stroked his neck and his silky ears. In my parents' room, the dog had torn the bedding and blankets from the bed and dug a wide hole right through the mattress to the wooden box spring on my dad's side of the bed. The dog had been searching for my father.

And next door, in my room, all thirty-two Barbies were thrown from the bed and scattered on the carpet. They landed around the room as if they'd stumbled and fallen, some on top of each other, legs in the air, some leaning up against the wall and the desk, naked and exposed, half-clothed, shoes missing, wigs twisted sideways. A pile of three had landed on the heat register, already melting.

Oppenheimer Park looked just like this scene, people piled up as if they'd been tossed there, half-naked. The first time I saw this on a Sunday afternoon, and every time afterward when I stepped off the bus, I thought of my dog and that day—the day such a great and terrible fear must have swept through our house, with hurricane force. There was nothing left to do but lie in the hole, trembling, breathing, waiting for someone to come.

When I arrived that first day in Vancouver's Eastside, and every day afterward, I had a strange, familiar longing stirring inside of me. I kept wishing, kept trying to believe that someone would step out from some-where, someone strong like my father had been that day, and call out to the people lying there, *It's okay, you'll be okay.*

This, I knew, was what Jesus had come for, to teach us to step in to such a nightmare, to be strong for the people who were not.

So I rode the busses and walked the streets, past churches with locked iron gates and the smell of urine on the steps. In the midst of it all, I talked to God inside my head. I had so many questions.

Why don't you just step in?

Why don't you stand up right now, in the middle of the street, in the middle of this raging storm, and still it?

Most often, before going home, I would stop at the Ovaltine Café on East Hastings for a cup of coffee, but one day I kept going for no reason at all. I didn't stop at the Ovaltine that day—instead I kept walking. I realized, after a block or two, I'd left my watch at home. It was getting dark and I wondered what time it was.

I looked for someone to ask, but there was no one on the street, not a single person. I kept walking, looking for the next open shop or café. It was nearly two blocks before I saw the shape of a person moving in a window a few shops away behind darkened glass, nearly like a ticket sales booth but older and dirtier. It was a hostel, I saw then. The attendant would be able to tell me the time. I knocked politely on the darkened glass to get his attention, and when the man slid up the glass covering to talk to me, I looked up into a face I knew instantly—the face of Mr. Diakiw.

I could not speak when he lifted the glass.

Mr. Diakiw.

Oh my God.

He didn't recognize me.

I stood there speechless, staring up at him in the little booth, his red hair still wild but thinning and greying. I was overcome by sadness, like I'd found the body of a man who'd been lost, like an uncle who had once been close to me and then disappeared at sea. I don't know why I didn't hate him; after everything that had happened at Austin Road Elementary,

I don't know why I didn't want to grab his red hair and yank his face through the window.

What I felt was sadness, like a cup of tea gone cold.

"Mr. Diakiw?" I said. "Is your name Wendell Diakiw?"

He sat back a little and looked confused, maybe scared.

"It's me," I said. "Heather Young."

"Oh, for God's sake, Heather," he said. "Oh, for God's sake."

It was exactly the way he used to say it at school and at piano lessons. Oh for God's sake. Oh for God's sake.

"I can't believe it," I said. And I couldn't. I wondered everything at once: Why isn't he in jail? Has he escaped? Should I call the police? Should I run?

But all I said was, "What are you doing here?"

I was shocked at how suddenly close I felt to this man. Of course I knew he was the terrible man who'd done terrible things to the boys we all knew, but for some reason it didn't—right at that moment—seem to matter.

He couldn't even speak, at first. He just stared out at me.

I saw him thinking, maybe wondering about slamming the window shut, but then he took a breath and sighed, sitting deep in his chair.

"I'm here doing Community Service Hours." He tried to smile a little.

"Oh."

Silence.

"Wow," I said. "You look just the same. I can't believe it."

Silence.

"I can't believe it either," he said.

Our eyes stopped and reached for each other at that moment, in a forsaken, dreaming kind of way. We stared into each other's eyes and I felt myself touch my childhood. In that moment I saw scenes flashing through my mind: me dancing across the stage in the *Pirates of Penzance* to Mr. Diakiw's piano; Jimmy and I trick-or-treating at his house on Halloween, each of us grabbing two huge handfuls of whatever we wanted from the basket of goodies; the whole class giggling at his jokes in choir practice; me trembling and apologizing for slamming the lid of his shining grand piano by accident.

I was almost wishing to hug him right then, because the man I knew and the man who'd gone to prison convicted of terrible things seemed to be two different people.

There was nothing more we could have said there, me on the street, him working behind the glass.

"Well, I'd better get back to work," he said.

"Yes, I'd better get my bus," I heard myself say.

"You take care."

"You too."

I walked off down the street.

But about three blocks away I stopped. I had questions. I needed to talk to him. I needed to understand. So I turned around and went back, running down the street, waving up at him again through the glass.

"Would you like to meet me for coffee sometime?" I said when he lifted the glass. "I'd really like to talk to you." Because I wanted to know, I wanted answers. The kids who'd gone to Austin Road Elementary deserved answers. How could I just walk away?

"Oh. Good grief." He fumbled with his hair the way I remembered he often did. "Oh, Heather." He stared at me, shaking his head, no.

"It's okay if you don't want to. I just thought we could talk."

He stared down at me through the glass.

I promised him with my eyes that it would be okay.

"That would be nice," he said, but I wasn't sure that he meant it. "How about tomorrow afternoon? I'm finished here at noon."

We agreed to meet at the large restaurant on the water that was shaped to look as if it were made of white sails. The ceiling was as high as the sails of a tall ship. Enormous fans forced the air past white flags that hung on every post, waving, waving in the fabricated breeze.

He saw me waiting at the table already and came over, looking as if he was intentionally in a hurry even though we were both early. I tried not to look surprised that he'd come. I was pleased to see him, but nervous, discovering I had nothing to say.

We talked about the weather and waited for the coffee to be served. I took a long time tearing open the sugar, stirring, finding a napkin to wipe the ring of coffee spilled in the saucer.

"How've you been?" I asked then quite suddenly.

"Well, I've got *nothing* at the moment if that's any indication. I don't own anything anymore, so I'm making do with a card table and a few boxes and some mismatched dishes. Not that I need much more, mind you; I don't do very much other than work at the hostel."

He tried to make it seem like a joke, but I forgot to be polite and laughed because I remembered the enormous grand piano that once stood in the studio in his house. I thought about his cardboard boxes and wondered where his cat went while he was in jail. I wondered if they sold the trains.

"So how long were you in jail for?" I said, trying to keep the conversation honest.

"Four years. Now I'm partway through thirty-six months of community service. That's why I'm at the hostel." He talked about the hostel for a while. He told me the names of the staff people, the guards, someone called Fred who worked opposite him and left everything in a mess. He got started on a story about Fred and one of the other staff people and I stopped listening while he talked.

He seemed older, simpler, noticeably diminished. I could almost no longer imagine him as the musician, the reckless red-headed prankster, the life of every community party, leading the school productions, challenging the principal in the hallway. He seemed to belong eating dinner on a cardboard box and being busy at a hostel. I almost wondered if he would pull out a mouse from his pocket and feed it sunflower seeds.

I couldn't tell if he was just filling in the time with empty words or if he was sharing his life with me. The effect, however, was the same: there was no space to talk about what happened back then.

I decided to make space.

"So, I never followed the case in detail, but I was wondering if there were lots of incidents with other boys after we grew up? You know, if it kept up across the years, is what I mean."

He seemed to appreciate me being direct.

"Oh it went on for awhile, sure. There were a few, but not as many as when you guys were younger. Things changed so much, you couldn't get away with anything anymore—and I don't mean just sexual things, I mean everything started to change. You couldn't get away with even a tap on someone's bottom in broad daylight in the middle of class! You had to be so careful after the laws started to change."

I just nodded, not knowing what else to say.

"You know, I mean, mostly it was no big deal. We played around a bit, but it was mostly just light and fun, nothing serious. God, no. Not after all the laws changed. Good heavens." He said it as if it was unthinkable, as if it was ridiculous to have even considered it after the laws had tightened up.

And I began to understand the picture from his perspective: there were only ever a few boys who were seriously involved; the others he just played around with—no big deal.

But there was one thing I really needed to know. It was the one thing I realized at that moment I had come to ask him: I needed to know if he was sorry.

For some reason I had been hoping—and not just hoping, believing—that he was sorry. I believed he would be. I had the picture already in my head: he was sorry, and I would find a way to forgive him, to make some step toward reconciliation. I would go home and tell them all: he was better now, that it had all been a mistake; that he hadn't meant to do what he'd done. If I could get this straight, perhaps we could wrap it all up, undo all that had been done, make things better.

So I took a breath and asked him.

"Do you regret it?" I said, waiting an eternity for the answer that would make it all a terrible mistake.

"Do I regret it?"

The waiter poured him a refill. He stirred his coffee and the waiter brought over more cream. There was enough silence to let him think.

"Oh Heather, I don't know—do I regret the whole mess? Yes, of course I do!"

"No, but what I mean is, are you *sorry*?"

"Good heavens—I don't know. Yes, I guess so—for some of the boys. You know for some who really got emotionally hurt, like little Ted McGuire, dear God, I regret that. You know he had no father, so he really got attached. I mean, it really hurt him I think."

I said nothing, waiting for him to fill the silence. He was thinking.

"But not the boys who really just enjoyed it—no. I'm not sorry for that."

I felt at that moment that I might actually vomit right there on the bench in the white sails restaurant. I saw the white flags waving at me, whispering *surrender.*

"Oh," I said. "Well, thanks for being honest, I guess."

I felt myself reach up and grip the cold hand of the moon and hold on tightly.

"It seems like a long time ago," he said.

I don't remember the rest of the conversation. Something about prison, something about community service, and then he glanced at his watch a few times, reaching for his menthol cigarettes.

I stood to hug him good-bye. I don't know why.

It was forced but necessary. I'd kept my word. Good-bye.

20

After I'd seen Mr. Diakiw, I called my brother; I wouldn't tell him about the visit, but I needed to hear his voice. Jimmy had not yet come right out and told me about Mr. Diakiw. Not directly, but I knew. Before the trial the police had called and asked him to testify. He told them he had nothing to say. When he'd hung up the phone, he was angry. Nothing had happened to him, that was for fucking sure. Years would pass before he would tell us the truth.

"They can go to hell with their questions," he'd said. Others had agreed to testify and that was enough.

I called him from a pay phone at Regent. He sounded clear-headed. We talked about his dog, his painting, his wife. They were trying to work things out it seemed.

"We're going to a couples thing at the church," he said finally, "with Pastor Bill."

"Really?" I was shocked. No one had told me that.

"Yeah, the same people we went to the marriage classes with."

"What's it like?"

"Good, nice people. I don't think anyone actually goes to church there, but they're nice people." It was a good sign, I thought.

"Have you talked to the guy who wrote that book yet?"

Was he interested or just making conversation? It was hard to tell.

"Not yet," I said. "I haven't really had a chance; it's kind of a hard thing to bring up in passing conversation."

He was silent, maybe disappointed.

"How are things?" I said.

"Not good."

"What do you mean?"

"You know what I mean." And I did.

"I'll be home soon." Did I think that would be some kind of consolation?

"You're better off there."

I didn't respond.

"Things are happening to me. Fucked up things."

"Have you gone back to the doctor?"

He laughed a cynical laugh. "They don't know anything about this; they can't do a fucking thing."

What could I say? Maybe he was right. What could I do? How far would I go with this chase for answers? And what, really, is the difference between chasing and fleeing? Does it make any difference if you are running toward something or away from something? In the end it may not matter. The streambed holds the water.

❧

It was true. I hadn't talked to Michael Green yet. But Regent, I'd learned since, was not a place I would learn about demons. It was meaningfully academic, but it was not a place to learn how to face the dark places I wondered about. Michael Green and that book of his were not typical of Regent academics; I'd never heard him speak about it.

He had a following at Regent, students who knew his work and his writing, who had followed him from a distance for years and then finally came to Regent to study because of him. When Michael Green came from England to Regent, he brought his own assistant to manage his schedule. She booked his calendar two years in advance; a flock of students swarmed around him whenever I saw him.

In contrast, I had never heard of him before I found that book; I wasn't in awe of him—I just needed information. He had plenty of people in awe of him—I just needed his help.

But I couldn't just walk up to him and say, "Hello, I'm a new student here and I'm wondering if you could help me sort out whether or not my brother has a demon living inside of him and, if so, what I should do about it?"

But later that week, in Michael's lecture on *Acts for Today*, a student raised his hand and asked a question. He was a fresh-out-of-Bible-School student.

"So what's your take on why we don't see that same kind of power operating in the world today?" he said. "Like the power we see in Acts— healings, deliverance, demons, all that kind of thing. What are your thoughts about that?"

This was a loaded theological question, and we all knew it.

The class sat on the edge of their seats waiting for him to answer. It was already 9:35 p.m. and class was over, but not one person got up to leave. Everyone wanted this answer.

He thought carefully and then laid it out.

"I don't think what you're saying is true, actually," the Reverend Dr. Michael Green answered him, pacing the floor at the front slowly, his hands clasped behind his back as he considered his response.

"I think you're wrong," he said to the student. "We are seeing the Spirit working in powerful ways in many parts of the world, not in North America perhaps, but all you have to do is go to Africa or South America and be with the churches there for a few days, and you'll see what I mean. The Spirit is alive and well, rest assured!" He spoke with passion.

Justin, a man from Kenya, called out, "Preach it, brother."

Then the students in the theatre who were from Africa, South America, and Central America applauded, stomping their feet. This was their territory now; this was something they knew.

I had an altogether different reaction.

I wasn't cheering.

All you have to do is go to Africa? or South America? I felt my insides crushing. How could that be? I'd come *here* for answers. *Here,* to Regent College. *This* was where I needed answers to be. He might as well have said I'd find the help I needed on Mars.

Michael took the challenge, read the crowd. If there'd been a stage to stand on, he'd have leapt up to it. He was just getting started.

"Do you know what's wrong with the Western Church today?"

He scanned the theatre looking for any takers who'd raise their hand. There were none.

"It's right here, right in this theatre!" he said, his hand sweeping the audience, implicating us all. He was a tiny leprechaun of a man, but at that moment he seemed to grow taller as his voice boomed.

"Look at us! Look around the room, here!" He demanded this.

Everyone glanced around, knowing we were being led down the garden path but unable to see what was coming.

"In this institution we have gathered some of the best young minds in the body of Christ on the planet today. In this very room! The cream of the crop sits here, look at you all!" He was shouting, excitedly. "And what are we doing? You and your churches—perhaps with your parish's support—are spending thousands and thousands of dollars on textbooks and cappuccinos to ask the same questions the disciples were asking two thousand years ago!" He was firing on all eight cylinders. "If Jesus was here walking the planet today, he wouldn't have touched this place with a ten-foot pole!" he said, slamming the table with his fist.

No one said a word. The room was dead silent.

"The world is waiting, people! There are magnificent servants of the Kingdom answering these questions already, people who are busy *doing* this work in the world. They're not sitting in a comfortable university lecture theatre spending thousands of dollars pondering what *might* be required of them! They're out there doing it!"

His face was smiling, but he was not happy; his cheeks were reddened, pulsing, as if he'd cut open a river of ideas. There was no stopping him. This was off-the-record Michael Green.

I looked around the room at the faces of the people seated there, people whose names I hardly knew. What were their stories; what brought them here? How many people in that room had come, like me, not knowing where else to go, doing the only thing they knew how to do? How many people sitting in that lecture hall had, like me, just felt their hope fall out and crack on the ground?

There must have been fifty people there that night. Who was this Michael Green to sweep the lot of us into a dust pile because we'd done the thing we thought was the right thing to do? Who did he think he was, dismissing us all like that?

He made one last statement: "The world is full of need, people! Pay attention. Here you sit wanting your comfort more than you want to live out the truth. That's what's wrong with the Church!"

Suddenly, there was a heat in my chest as if a fire had been lit inside of me. Who did he think he was strutting back and forth up there? I wasn't there for comfort. I was there for help. I stood to my feet in the middle of the theatre, until he spotted me.

"Question?" he said, smiling aggressively.

"No, not a question. Just a comment."

I took a breath and let go.

"I'd like to challenge what you just said, actually. I think you're wrong about the people sitting here. You have no idea what our stories are in this room. You have no idea why we've come. You don't know what it's cost us to get here, and you don't know that we've come here to be comfortable instead of committed. I think you're wrong to suggest that. This room might be full of people who say to God everyday, *Here am I, send me*. You don't know until you know the stories of the people sitting in this room." I stood my ground, staring down the theatre at him. I had nothing to lose; I didn't need his connections or his good favor. I needed information, nothing more.

Michael Green said nothing at first. He just stared back at me.

"Right," he bent his head quizzically. "Well, then, perhaps you're right!" he smiled broadly, nodding and bowing with a dramatic sweep of his arms, a caricature of forced humility. There was something cunning in where this was going.

"What's your name, young lady?"

Young lady? Did he *really* just say that?

"My name is Heather," I said.

"Right then, Heather. What about you?"

His hands were on his hips, staring up at me, not quite smirking but almost, waiting to launch his gotcha moment.

"Are *you* willing? Would *you* go, like the disciples in Acts, would you pack up and go, say . . . tomorrow? What's holding you back?" He waited for my reply.

I didn't have to think. I knew the answer. Of course, I would. If he'd wanted to prove his point, he'd picked the wrong young lady.

"If God called me when I walked out of this room tonight," I said, "I would go *tonight*. That's why I'm here." And I meant it.

I did not sit down. I waited for his response.

"Good then!" he said. "Come see me Monday at lunch then, will you?"

"All right," I said. "I'll see you then."

Why did it feel like a duel?

He put his books in his briefcase abruptly and snapped it closed.

Class dismissed.

I decided not to get off the bus at my residence that night; I needed more time to think. I stayed on the bus until East Hastings and then walked along the top end, where it was still safe after dark. As I walked, the air was cool. I was aware of the world around me, the shouts and honks, the people sleeping in corners.

I thought about the end of the lecture, about what Michael Green was trying to say. And he was right in many ways, I knew that, but he'd been careless. What he'd said about Jesus was exactly right and I knew it. If Jesus *were* walking the streets of Vancouver, he would not be at Regent College. He would be on East Hastings Street, but he wouldn't just walk around like a fool, staring and thinking, doing nothing. He wouldn't just ride the bus; he would know exactly what to do.

21

It's hard to predict when you're standing in it, where a stream will eventually end up. When you're knee-deep in the current, water rushing through your legs, you can peer ahead only as far as the trees will allow, accounting for what seem to be the natural boundaries, mountains and obvious rises in landscape, for example. You don't see until you walk it, the sudden bend that will take the water somewhere you could never have imagined.

On Monday at noon I went upstairs to Michael Green's office.

His assistant, Janet, was there.

"Can I help you?" she said.

"I'm here to see Michael Green . . . ? He said to come today at noon."

"I don't have you in his diary, did you make an appointment?" She looked down at her book and flipped the pages.

"He just said to come." She smiled and raised her eyebrows a little.

"Hmm . . . well yes that does happen from time to time, he's such a busy a man, I'm sure he's forgotten. Perhaps make an appointment with me and I can enter it in his diary. How's next Thursday at ten o'clock?"

I'd waited all weekend, steeling myself for whatever Monday would bring; next Thursday was too far away.

Just then we heard footsteps flitting quickly up the stairs.

"Might be your lucky day." She looked amused.

"Ah yes, there you are! Sorry, I'm late, busy day, come in, come in, let's sit now, shall we?"

I followed him into his office. He motioned for me to sit.

He leaned back in his large leather chair, which seemed to swallow him.

I stared across the desk at him, taking it all in.

This was the man I'd come to meet. At last, here we were.

"Such steady brown eyes . . ." he said smiling, teasing me, noting my deep concentration, my earnest self, perched on the edge of the chair, waiting. I laughed, trying to look a bit less intense.

"So!" he said. "I've done a bit of poking around, and I'm suggesting Africa, Africa Enterprise in particular—they're a very good organization, Michael Cassidy is a great leader, and they do good work."

Was this a joke?

"They've got all kinds of needs at the moment, so I'm not sure of the details yet, but I've spoken to them and they're happy to have you."

Was this a test?

I'm sure we talked then but I don't remember. At least he must have talked. All I could hear was *Africa* echoing in my head.

He added one last thing: "It will cost about $6,000."

I shook my head and laughed.

"I don't have $6,000. I spent every penny I had to get *here*. To Regent."

"Well, don't let that stop you," he said dismissing my objection. "The Lord will find a way. It's still a couple of months away; they'll need you in June."

When I got off the bus near the residence I lived in, I didn't go home to my room. I went straight to the little Catholic church across the street, the place I went to pray. I don't think there was anyone in the church that afternoon, but I wouldn't have seen them if they'd been there. I went straight to the candles at the front and lit half a dozen. I must have thought that would help. I sat cross-legged on the floor in front of them, watching them flicker.

My head dropped to my chest. I was tired.

Were the answers in Africa? Was that what this was about? This was too much.

And I had no money; it was ridiculous. This was more than I could manage. I was tired; I was just so deeply tired of it all.

When I closed my eyes, I could almost feel the velvet curtain that hung behind the cross at the little church, soft on my neck, wrapping around my body. I lay down on the carpet.

I'm not sure how much time passed before I heard it, but at some point there was a voice, speaking clearly. *Come boldly*, it said, soft as a ribbon slipping through my fingers, *to the throne of grace and you will find help for what you need.* It was Hebrews 4:16.

The voice found me there asleep on the floor and pulled the velvet curtain up over my shoulders, whispering gently in my ear as I slept. It fell softly from some mysterious place, silent but clear. When I opened my eyes, it was dark outside. The traffic had quieted. It was nearly midnight; the candles had burned to a pool of wax, but I knew exactly what to do.

Come boldly, I repeated, as I climbed the stairs two at a time to Michael Green's office the next morning.

"Hi there!" I said to Janet. "Is Michael here?" I was out of breath from rushing.

"Do you have an appointment?" she said, not glancing up from what she was doing.

I told her I didn't, but that I would wait.

"Oh no, you can't just sit here, he's very busy today. "

"Yes, I know, I've brought a book. I'll sit outside his office and wait. I need to see him."

She sighed deeply.

A couple of hours passed but I wasn't leaving. *Come boldly to the throne of grace and you will find help for what you need.* The words floated before my eyes as I sat waiting. It's not what I need, I thought. It's what my brother needs. But still the strength behind the verse was what mattered. I certainly didn't need anything, but my brother did.

Why did I insist on this? Was there nothing I needed?

Come boldly and you will find help for what you need. I waited patiently for the sound of his steps, for the arrival of the man who would know what to do to help my brother.

This was my chance, while the stakes were high for both Michael Green and for me, while the friction in the lecture hall still lingered and we had yet to resolve it, while the sparring over what we were made of still mattered. I was willing, but was he? In a few days it wouldn't matter to the Reverend Dr. Green. He'd have moved past it, wouldn't even remember my name, this whole thing would be crowded from his mind.

I would wait, boldly.

Another hour passed. *Come boldly.*

Then I heard his footsteps and Janet warning him I was outside his office.

"She's been here for three hours. There's no escaping her, I'm afraid. "

He came rushing round the corner, forcing a smile and a warm greeting.

"I'm hoping for an unscheduled four minutes of your time. I promise not to take long."

"Yes, yes, of course, do come in!" He was polite.

His desk was overflowing with papers, he lifted a large pile of things from the chair and tossed them on the floor. "Sit down, please."

For a minute I lost all sense of where to start.

Come boldly.

I wasn't sure he remembered me; he looked puzzled.

"So you said to get back to you about Africa," I reminded him gently.

"Yes, of course, what have you thought about it all?"

He was in a hurry.

"I have one problem, which is the $6,000," I said. "But that's why I'm here. I need your help."

He nodded and took off his glasses, rubbed his eyes and then stared at me, giving me his full attention.

"Come boldly to the throne of grace," I repeated out loud for him. "So here I am, coming boldly. Michael, I'm wondering if you would come to my hometown, Prince George, to speak at a fundraising dinner to help me raise the money to go?"

I stared across the desk at him and didn't blink.

He said nothing.

For a long time.

He just stared.

Then he spoke. "Ah, those steady brown eyes . . ." he said, rubbing his hands together, gripping his fingers.

He leaned forward then, and nodded.

The world seemed to hush.

Was he considering it? I could see his brain working.

"It would be in a few weeks time." I said quickly. "I'll make all the arrangements so it's simple for you."

I could see he was thinking. Not sure at all what to say.

"Yes," he said. "I will come."

Neither of us looked away.

"When you have a date, tell Janet, and have her clear my schedule."

And before I could ask him, before I could figure out how to say it, he asked it himself: "Would it be all right if I stayed at your home, to meet your family?"

"Of course!" I said.

He was coming.

The one man in the world who could help my brother was actually coming.

When I'd booked the church, I called the printer and had them print the tickets. Then I called my brother.

"You will not believe this!" I said, dying to tell him.

The tickets sold out in five days. I had a waiting list of twenty-four by the next weekend. But I'd had a hard time concentrating on the fundraiser itself. I was distracted by Friday; Friday night meant more to me than the fundraiser.

On Friday night, Michael Green would meet Jimmy; on Friday night Michael Green would be in my house, sitting at the table with my brother.

"Jimmy, it's just dinner. You don't have to say anything!"

"I just don't want to talk about it," he said. "I don't even know the guy."

"Don't worry, you won't have to."

But I wasn't sure what would happen; neither of us were.

We stared across the table at each other.

I shrugged. "Can you believe it?" I said. "Can you believe the guy who wrote the book is actually coming *here*?"

"No. I can't." He shook his head and breathed out deeply.

But he was smiling. We both were.

Maybe this was *it*.

When the plane landed on Friday evening, I panicked. How would I explain in the short twenty-minute drive home what I needed from him? How could I explain about the book in the box at the church, about searching for help, and about my brother? How could I explain how much this meant to me?

He was cheerful but he was tired. I didn't have any idea what he'd had to go through to make room for this. He'd cancelled his commitment to speak at the opening of the Cathedral and important plans he'd had with his family.

What was I thinking? How could I drop this on him, just like that, just minutes before we'd arrive at my house, where Jimmy and the rest of my family were waiting?

But I did. There was no other way.

"I have to confess something to you," I began as he fastened his seatbelt.

"Confess away!" he tried to be jovial, but I could see it in his eyes, nothing more please, not now.

"It's a long story so I'll try to give you the short version. I read your book, *I Believe in Satan's Downfall*. Before I even went to Regent; it's the reason I went." I explained the rest as I drove.

"So," I said carefully, feeling guilty about the arrangement without having asked him. "I guess that's where you come in. He'll be at my parents' house with us for dinner."

"Goodness," he said. "Well, I shall look forward to meeting him. Sometimes it's not very straightforward."

Dinner was pleasant, everyone was well behaved, Jimmy was talkative. He sat across from Michael. They enjoyed a couple of beers while they chatted about his painting and so on. Absolutely ordinary.

By ten o'clock Michael looked exhausted. He excused himself and went up to bed; Jimmy and Uta went home. When the dishes were finished, I went upstairs and sat on the edge of my bed looking out my window over the sky of stars.

What had I been expecting? That Jimmy would fall on the ground frothing at the mouth? That Michael would pull a magic wand from his suitcase and fix everything? I didn't even remember anymore.

The next afternoon, on the way to the fundraiser, Michael raised the subject.

"Your brother." He looked thoughtful. "He's all right—a nice lad, drinks a bit much but there's nothing obvious to me. I'm not an expert on the subject—I just know what I've experienced."

We were quiet for a while.

"And you're bound to learn all about this in Zimbabwe, I would think. "

Yes, I realized. I was going to Zimbabwe.

That night we would raise all the money I needed and Michael himself would donate the cost of his airfare and then some.

The things he'd said about my brother were meant to be a comfort to me. And they should have been. But I had been hoping, I guess, for something unbelievable to happen, that Michael Green might pull some magic potion out of his hat and voilà—Jim would be fine.

It had not been real to me until then.

I really would be going to Africa.

Until that point, I thought it might have been enough to be willing.

22

In the rural areas of Zimbabwe, there aren't many cars and even fewer white people. If a white person in a car ever does come driving slowly down a dust road on the back edge of the townships, the children come running, red dust flying, quick black legs running fast, racing the car, leading the way, laughing, shouting, taunting, the bottoms of their feet flashing as they speed ahead.

I'd come for six months to work with African Enterprise, known locally as AE. I'd liked what I'd read about AE. They stood for reconciliation; they were committed to reconciliation between God and humanity, between divided races, between husbands and wives, between churches. African Enterprise was about restoring relationships that were broken. I believed in that.

I would be helping prepare for the organization's mission in Bulawayo, Zimbabwe's second largest city. The goal of the mission— *"Bulawayo for Jesus"*—was to bring people to the Lord, but also to support the churches to work together better in their own communities. AE brought in teams of people from all across Africa; in Zimbabwe, the churches were key providers of support for many families, in addition to being places of worship. I could invest myself in this, even if I'd come with my own agenda.

❧

I took in my first glimpse of the dry flat land from the plane. I could see the capital, Harare, in the distance, the surrounding land tufted with rocky outcrops and branchy trees reaching out and not up, toward the earth and not the sky. Their leaves were a cautious green, not quite silver but wishing to be. Zimbabwe had been in drought for seven years and the trees knew it. They knew something I didn't that day: the drought would not be lifting.

When I came into the arrivals area, there was no mistaking them: Chris and Helga Sewell, the team leader and his wife, had white skin, white hair, white clothes, and white teeth. Everyone else was black. That's how I remember it. The airport was busy with black people coming and going, pushing bags and lining up to get on airplanes.

Chris and Helga introduced themselves, then embraced me with stiff British hugs and pointed toward the door where I would meet them when I'd found my backpack.

The air was steamy, rich with the smell of the bodies. It reminded me all at once of moss and autumn and chocolate. It would settle into the back of my throat and I would recognize it from then on, breathing it in secretly in grocery store lines and in churches, in chicken buses and hot bread shops. I would breathe it in like the incense that filled the chapel at the convent in Mission where I'd stayed on reading break that year.

When you cross the world and begin a new life in an unfamiliar place, however temporary, something happens to the substance of time, each hour is stretched long, covering vast amounts of landscape, like the long shadows of trees when the sun is low. Each hour somehow covers the space of a week and when just a day in that new place has passed, you can see it in your eyes already; when an entire month has passed, you hardly recognize yourself.

We tend to think travel is about seeing things you've never seen. But it's the leaving that counts. When you truly leave the place you know, you become someone new.

I had found my own accommodation in the city of Bulawayo by asking around. I couldn't bear the thought of living with the white church families that had offered me a couch to sleep on; I was shocked by the way they treated the black Zimbabweans.

My roommate was Patty, a young professional Ndebele woman. We shared a small apartment in downtown Bulawayo, walking distance to everything. Even so, I was grateful for the car the local mission team had loaned me. Patty was tall and beautiful; her skin was like velvet, her voice wise. She taught businesses how to install and use accounting software for an international software firm.

"Just leave your washing in the basket. Elizabeth will take of it," Patty said on her way out the door.

"Oh no," I said. "I can manage."

Who was Elizabeth, I wondered.

"No, really, that's the way we do it. That's her job," Patty said.

"That's her job?"

"Yes," she said. "She does the cleaning and the laundry. She comes a few days a week, but we do our own dishes."

I was astonished. I had seen the class and racial divide on my first day in Zimbabwe and I'd been thankful to escape. But I hadn't expected it here. White Zimbabweans typically thought of themselves as Rhodesians still—faithful to England and superior in every way. No one would have used the word *slave,* but it was the only word that came to my mind during those first days.

On my first day in Zimbabwe, Mrs. Sewell, who was going for tea to Midsummer Hill Manor, had asked if I'd be interested in joining her. The De Swardt family was an important family in the church; they were one of the largest donors. I'd been pleased to be asked to go along; there was so much I wanted to see. Everything was interesting for me that day, the color of the earth, the thick vines that covered the walls surrounding the properties, disguising the spikes that stood guard along the top, the sparkling blue pool that Chris said would be ready soon, the cool, musty smell of the rooms in the Sewells' brick home, the way heavy curtains hung gracefully in every room. There were rooms for sitting in, for dining in, for receiving guests in.

"Perhaps by the time you're back, Kennedy will have the pool ready," Chris had said, kissing his wife on the cheek.

"Is Kennedy your son?" I asked Helga as we pulled out the driveway.

"Oh," Helga laughed, "Goodness no, he's our gardener."

Kennedy and his family of five lived in the back garden in a shed. Four children under five years of age moved silently, fearfully behind the fence that kept them hidden.

At Midsummer Hill Manor, morning sun filtered through the spray of the garden hose when we pulled up in front of the staircase. The lawn held droplets of water for a moment or two, before the heat of the day devoured them. In Zimbabwe the grass is coarse and sharp edged, it's not the kind of grass you would throw yourself on just to feel the earth under your body. It's not the kind of grass your fingers would move freely through searching for a four-leaf clover.

There was a black man watering the Jacaranda tree by the gate. He glanced at the ground quickly, turning his head when we approached so that he didn't look at us. I wanted to say hello, but I understood without being told that this might be the wrong thing to do.

Helga walked past the man without even seeming to notice he was there. I followed her but smiled silently at him, hoping to catch his eye.

He was looking at the ground, on purpose.

"How lovely to see you, dahling!" said Mrs. De Swardt, greeting us at the top of the stairs. She spoke in a strong accent that I had not yet begun to recognize as Afrikaans. She reached to kiss Mrs. Sewell's cheek. After introductions we sat in the lounge room in stiff white chairs for morning tea, with proper china and fresh milk.

"Ask Florence to be sure it's *fresh* milk, Melissa—this morning's milk, please Melissa."

Melissa, who must have been ten years old, brought in the tea and helped to serve it. We talked about many things, amounting mostly to nothing: the weather, the mission in Bulawayo, a new pastor at one of the local churches, the garden, the heat of the sun already this year.

Soon, Mrs. De Swardt bent to pour a second cup of tea, but there was no more hot water. Her face reddened, rage filled her eyes; she was deeply embarrassed, apologizing for her daughter's deplorable behavior, her wretched spoiling of the morning.

I couldn't bear to look at Melissa.

With a slow, certain voice, hideously controlled, she turned to Melissa.

"Melissa—do not ever, *ever* serve without an extra pot of hot water." She did not shout. She didn't have to. "Is that clear?"

"I'm sorry, mummy. May I be excused?" She waited for her mother's answer, tears brimming the lids of her eyes.

After some time, when Mrs. De Swardt had held her there long enough to establish her authority, she answered, "You may."

Rules are rules, I thought as she left the room, graceful but broken. Rules are rules.

When we were leaving, I saw the gardener raking at the edge of a floral garden. I waved and smiled. He smiled back with such a grand toothy smile it made me happy. He dropped the rake trying to wave back to me but managed to grab it, fearfully, before it clattered on the footpath.

"Oh yes," said Mrs. Sewell, "That's Lazarus." She nodded politely in his direction and turned away, seeming to want to lead by example.

So when Elizabeth arrived at the flat I would share with Patty, I could have mistaken her for an auntie, not the help. She was friendly and loving, older than Patty and I; the sun had creased her face so it was hard to tell her age. She was outgoing and talkative. At first she did a lot of bowing when she spoke to me, as if I was royalty. She was a great woman of faith, as well, and thanked Jesus out loud for everything.

When a few weeks had passed, she stopped bowing and instead reached to hug me close to her, then paused to hold my face in her hands for a moment while she looked up to heaven and muttered something to Jesus, something motherly. I'd wished she'd been my auntie.

Finally I got the courage to ask her.

"Elizabeth, why do you do this? Why are you cleaning for Patty and I?"

Why it was not obvious to me even then, I still don't understand.

"Oh my dear," she patted my leg. She understood why I was asking. "Patty is a very good boss; she pays me well, yes, she does. I need this job so badly, you know my honey."

She held my hands in hers.

"My daughter and her childrens, you know they need the help from me too. My husband, he is not a good husband, not the kind for nice girls like you. But I take care of him. And I am so lucky to have this job. I don't want to work in the factory; I like to see my babies. I like to come home before they sleep so I can see my babies. So I clean and do the washing as best I can and always more and Patty, she pays me more than she should. She's a good boss to me that's for sure; and you, too, of course. I am so lucky. The Lord looks after me always and always. And I pray for you too, the Lord will look after you."

After that I always left an extra envelope for Elizabeth in the washing. She took it home to her babies and prayed for me "all the day and night," she said.

23

I needed every last one of Elizabeth's prayers.

Yes, I was in the middle of an adventure in Africa, but the endless hours of mindless work with no real progress toward the answers I'd come for was draining. The majority of the work set aside for me to do for the first month involved photocopying and hanging posters around town. Every day. Then a lot of sitting and waiting, and more sitting and waiting. Occasionally I would be asked to lick and seal envelopes, and this was always a welcome change. The work was not what I'd expected.

I understood that Chris was behind in his own work, and I could see he was not great at delegating what needed to be done. In time, however, I found ways to use my skills and strengths. Chris grew confident enough to shift the responsibilities of the townships to my plate.

It was more difficult for him to work with churches in the townships. I came as a white person, yes, but as a Canadian. It was easier for people to forget the old Rhodesia with a white Canadian. I felt at ease in the townships. I wondered if the same would be true of me in Canada, if I would be able to step so easily away, as a white person, from the memories the First Nations communities carried.

The younger black pastors in the townships were accepting. We worked hard together as a team making preparations for the ten-day event that was fast approaching. The township churches were not places

141

for elite groups of worshippers; they were the gathering places of the community without barriers of class. Everyone, it seemed, found a way to get by and to make sure the neighbors did too. The churches were authentic in a way that made me think of Jesus.

In addition, I got busy in my travels about town with posters, trying to find out more about the power that Michael Green and the other students had talked about. Here I was, in the midst of the place that held the secrets of power over evil spirits, and I'd found out nothing more.

I asked Patty one evening. We were eating dinner, and she was embarrassed at my interest. She knew how it sounded to me, from Canada, but she also knew what was true for her and true in Zimbabwe.

"Why do you want to know about all of this rubbish?" she said, half annoyed and half smiling.

"I'm just curious about it." I didn't tell her about my brother.

Patty was a strong, intelligent woman, sophisticated and independent. She was engaged to marry Densen, a physics professor at the university. Denson had earned his master's degree at Cornell in New York.

Patty did not grow up in the bush like her sisters and brother. She grew up at her auntie's house in town. She was the chosen child, the one who was sent to school. I could see why—her mind was quick; she worked hard. The rest of her family stayed in Filabusi, a few hours drive into the middle of the bushed areas. There are no real roads in Filabusi, mostly dust tracks to follow. Patty's family lived in a small baked-mud hut, growing maize, cooking on a fire, keeping a few chickens and goats nearby. Patty looked after them as best she could.

When we visited, we brought a box of baby chicks and a large bag of feed as a gift. Twice a day we walked half a mile to get water and carry it home on our heads. The truth is, I didn't carry anything on my head but an empty water bucket and I held it there just long enough for the picture. My neck felt damaged just from the empty jug. The tiny little eight-year-old girls could carry twice what I could.

Patty's father died when she was young. He died of a curse put on him by a witch. This is what I asked her about again.

"Yes, a witch." She said it again to be sure I understood she meant it. "A witch put a curse on my father. We don't know why. Maybe she wanted our land, or someone else wanted the land and paid her. We don't know."

"How did she do that?"

"I don't know—she just did. It made him very sick."

"Did he go to the doctor?"

"Yes, but the doctors can't do anything about curses, not at a hospital!" she laughed at me, shaking her head. It was the way my brother had laughed.

"He went to see the Inyanga a few times; he tried to help him, gave him some special medicine, *muti*, but it was too late, the curse was already killing him." The Inyanga is a traditional healer. Some people call them witchdoctors.

Everything in Zimbabwe has spiritual roots, bad things and good things, and they usually begin in another world. When people run out of water, have an accident, meet their partner, or fall pregnant, the cause most often is in the spiritual world, with the dead or the fallen.

So as the weeks of preparation continued, I hoped for some new knowledge I could take home with me. I sometimes wondered about the singing. When evening had set in and the sweet smell of wood fires filled the air, in the distance I could sometimes hear the voices of Africans singing. There was nothing in the world I could compare that to. Maybe the sound of the singing was filled with enough beauty to take on the darkest night, I thought. Even if the moon fell out of the sky one day, these voices would nearly be enough.

A few days before the mission was to begin, I scanned the schedules and reviewed the training sessions. I felt pleased. We'd scheduled speakers and support teams for all eight venues and had leaders at each to take charge of the site. We had a well-organized team of people to take care of the townships, led in part by Pastor Usavi, Pastor Nyahti, and Pastor Mangwende. African Enterprise had called in more staff for the mission. There were people coming from South Africa, Swaziland, Zambia, Botswana, and Mozambique.

"Norma David is coming, she's walking now," someone reported at a gathering in Luveve Township.

"Now?" I said stunned. "She's walking?" I wondered who Norma David was.

"Everyone is walking," Pastor Usavi said. "Some people will walk for days to get here; some will walk a week."

I was surprised.

"But how do people even know about this?"

"They know. It's very important to the people. Norma David will be here tomorrow."

"Who's Norma David?" I said.

"Who is Norma David? You don't know?"

I shook my head. "Should I?"

"She's a very important woman to the people. She is connected to God. When she speaks, she speaks from God. Everyone knows this."

They went on to explain: Norma David had been a key guerilla fighter, a leader in the war. Since then, she'd become a spiritual advisor to Robert Mugabe, Zimbabwe's president. When she felt he must be given a message from God, she went straight to his house and demanded to see him. He would welcome her. Mugabe was seen by many as a thief who looked out for himself and his cronies.

"Does she support Mugabe?"

"No, but he knows he must be kind to her. He knows how important she is to the people."

"How does she even know when to come?" I asked, amazed at how messages spread across the country like that.

"Everyone knows. They are all coming."

24

When people in Zimbabwe ask me about Canada, I feel the distance. I can feel that I am 16,000 kilometers from home just by the way they say it. *Kahanadah.* They ask if there is snow in *Kahanadah*, and it stops me every time, the way the name of my country sounds foreign.

These are the things my family in *Kahnahdah* doesn't tell me: that Jimmy is in the hospital; that he's been having seizures and convulsions; that the world is spinning out of control for them all. They don't tell me he has gone to detox a few times and has been hospitalized on the psych ward for several days. They don't tell me that the ambulance has come for him three times, that the psychiatrists are baffled, that he is dangerously depressed, and that no one seems to know what they can do.

So while I am busy getting the township details organized for the mission, my brother is slowly dying. Later, my family in *Kahnahdah* will tell me they didn't want to worry me.

I hadn't made many inroads into solving the problem I'd come to solve. Admittedly, I had been busy with work for Africa Enterprise, but it was more difficult than I'd expected. There were challenges I hadn't counted on in Bulawayo. The Church in Zimbabwe is comparatively conservative and dominated by men. It was a cautious walk to work closely with a team of black pastors—all men—suspicious of "American ways." For some church leaders, the fact that I was a white woman working with black men in the townships was proof enough. Women like me were loose and reckless; the Church was guarded. A few of the older pastors refused to speak to me at all and sent their wives to meet me instead.

I can only imagine the gossip around town when I ran in the evenings, wearing long shorts and an oversized t-shirt. Christian women were covered here; they didn't run and they didn't wear shorts. But I wasn't giving up; I was here, in the heart of the place that would know how to free my brother, and I'd come a long way for this.

The team of men I worked with in the townships had, I felt, moved beyond all of this. We were colleagues now . . . and friends. Perhaps they'd been nervous at first, but not anymore. After one of the meetings, I overheard a few of them talking about sinfulness. After weeks of working together, I'd come to know them well enough to ask candid questions.

Pastor Nyahti was the pastor of a church that insisted their members wear sports coats with no split in the back of the jacket.

I asked him to repeat that—I was sure I'd heard him wrong.

He said it again. It was sinful to wear a sports coat with a slit in the back. This, he assured me, was a sign of sinfulness; it was dangerous even. The same was true of ladies' dresses. No slits were permitted. This, apparently, was how sin got in.

I couldn't help laughing, but he took it goodheartedly.

"Are you serious?" I said. "You can't be serious!"

"Don't laugh—it's true. Many of the women and men in our churches became possessed by demons because of this. And it's not just our church, there are others. We have to deliver many of our people in Zimbabwe from demons that have gotten in this way."

This was my chance. I asked him about deliverance.

"I'd like to go to one of the deliverance services sometime," I said, my interest sparked. I imagined trying to explain this all to my brother, certain his problem had nothing to do with a slit in his sports coat.

"Of course," he said. "Tomorrow night there is a service at Pastor Mangwende's church. We were just talking about this. You know him?"

I did know him, but I was surprised because so far everything about Pastor Mangwende had been silent. He almost never spoke. He was shy around me. He seemed to be the youngest of the pastors, closest to my age, a small man with a boyish face.

At the deliverance service, Pastor Mangwende was there assisting, praying over a woman at the front of the church, his hands were on her head at first, then slid down to her throat as she called out. He prayed in words I didn't understand, unsure if he was speaking in tongues or in Ndebele. He was working with a visiting healer from Zambia.

The Zambian man walked through the church until he found someone he could see, with his spiritual eyes, had a demon. She was seated in the back of the hall. He asked her to come forward.

The rest of the deliverance was much like I'd seen at the Pentecostal church back home. I couldn't hear much of what was being said at the front, but the woman was crying. When Pastor Mangwende shouted out, "In Jesus's name, come out!" the woman began shaking and screaming. He shouted it again, maybe three times, and each time the woman shook more, until at last she fell to the ground. When she sat up a few minutes later, she had been delivered. She seemed not to know what had happened.

I tried not to feel disappointed.

25

The night before the mission began, I was late to the Welcome Dinner, the opening event, but it didn't matter; in a room of 150 people, you ought to be able to slip in a bit late. The hall was noisy and buzzing with people I'd never seen. The mission teams had arrived, but I was tired and planned to leave as soon as dinner was finished. I needed some rest.

There was a long lineup for food, so I got in the queue. A very short and stocky, barefooted African woman stood in front of me in the line. She was so short I could look easily over her head at the buffet; I was senselessly hungry. I didn't even see her turn around and look up at me.

"Ai!" she shouted up to get my attention, her eyes flashing.

She was loud and pushy.

"Hello," I said, startled.

She stared up at me and held my eyes.

"It's a good thing this is a slow line for your sake," she said.

I smiled, hoping not to start a conversation. I was hungry.

"Did you hear what I just said?" She looked perplexed. "I said, it's a good thing the line is slow, not for me but for you."

"Why is that?" What an odd woman.

"I have some news for you."

I was not at all interested. If I'd messed up someone's schedule or double booked a hall, I didn't want to know about it until after I'd had something to eat. I smiled and said nothing.

"Don't you want to know it?"

"I'm not sure; it's been a long day."

"I will tell you anyway." She scanned the room, looking for someone. She was short so she didn't see him right away. When he stood up to let someone slip past him, she spotted him.

"Ai!" she said, pointing to the man. "Do you see that nice boy over there? The tall, handsome one?"

There was a tall fellow about my age next to Chris Sewell. He was one of the international students with the Discipleship Training School at a farm twenty kilometers out of town, a "Youth With a Mission" base.

"The boy by Chris?" I said. "Why?"

"You are ready for this?" she said giggling, glowing a little.

She paused to make sure I was paying attention, then blurted it out: "He is your husband!"

I smiled and shook my head; she'd mistaken me for someone else.

"No," I explained. "I'm not married."

"Not for long!" She slapped her thigh, laughing.

She was enjoying this.

"It's true," she said, shrugging her shoulders. "I will make your wedding dress if you like. I can make *veerrry* beautiful wedding dresses. You just tell me, before I go home. I can measure you later this week. But not tomorrow, I am not in town tomorrow."

I laughed because she was so odd, and she seemed to be enjoying this so much. I glanced over at the tall fellow who was now sitting next to Chris. What a funny woman.

"When God chooses a husband for you, it's nothing to laugh about," she said stone-faced, perhaps accusing me.

I could see, then, that she was actually dead serious; my laughing offended her.

"You know who I am?" she asked, reaching for the tongs to serve herself chicken.

"No, I'm sorry, I should have introduced myself. I'm Heather. . . ."

She passed me the tongs, interrupting me. "I know who you are, but do you know who *I* am?"

She watched me, thinking.

"You go and see Mr. Chris Sewell, okay? With that tall, handsome boy. You go on over now and ask Mr. Chris Sewell who am I. Okay? Then you come to see me about your dress."

She turned and made her way to a table on the other side of the room.

What an odd woman. I had nowhere else to sit, so I made my way over to Chris. He stood and waved me over when he saw me coming.

"Welcome! How do you like it?" He swept his hand around the room, reminding me to pause and take it all in. I was overwhelmed, actually. It had been a lot of work.

There were dozens of people at tables laughing and eating. The white pastors had made a point of sitting at tables with people they didn't know, mostly black pastors and speakers. The team from South Africa had arrived; Michael Cassidy, the founder of African Enterprise, was busy in the corner talking intently to a group from Harare. Christopher Moyo and a few women from Nketa Baptist Church sat with a group from Mpompoma. Even the older pastors who had refused to speak to me as a single, white woman had come. Everyone was lively and enthusiastic, talking excitedly.

This is what joy sounds like, I thought. This is what the Great Banquet sounded like in my mind, the way I'd imagined it from the felt-board stories.

"We've done it!" He smiled and hugged me with one arm around my shoulders.

It felt good to be there.

"Sit, sit, sit," he said, realizing I'd still been organizing details and hadn't eaten yet.

Then he turned to the young man beside him, who was looking up at me.

"Do you know James?"

I smiled and nodded.

"Hi," James said.

"Yes, we've met," I said to Chris, then turned to James. "How are things going out at the farm?"

I sat down, hoping James would talk so I could eat. I guessed he was Australian by his accent. We chatted for a few minutes until he excused himself to find the rest of his team.

"Bye," I said, but he was already gone.

"Chris," I said, scanning the room looking for the woman; she was by the dessert table. "Do you see that woman over there, the little one by the desserts?"

"Yes . . ." he said, raising his eyebrows.

"Who is she? She said you'd know."

"I do know, of course." He looked puzzled. "She is Norma David. She's a powerful woman; you want her on your side." He laughed but he meant it. "They say she speaks for God. Truly, she's an extraordinary woman." He shrugged, smiling. "She's tough. Guerilla warrior. Says exactly what she thinks. Even to Mugabe."

I watched her carefully.

"Why do you ask?"

"No reason, just curious. She said to ask you."

I scanned the room for James.

"That's odd. I wonder why she said I'd know her."

Yes, I thought. Very odd.

After dinner, I reviewed the schedules quickly so I could distribute them. Every venue needed two support people, coordinators who would help at the hall. I'd planned to be at Nketa Hall on my own; I knew most of the people out there already so I didn't need help. But when I looked at the paper in my hand, the roster for Nketa Hall, I changed my mind.

Instead of leaving the line beside my name blank, I wrote in *James*.

When you're running, it doesn't matter what forest you're in, the trees blur. The sun darts behind every tree you pass, watching. When you're running through a forest, you don't notice the rough, corky bark of an older fir or the sap bubbles forming on a young, smooth limb. When you're running, you miss the tiny white flowers on the ground cover that dangle like bells, you miss the patterns of light in the leaves overhead. But for a time the blur is soothing, for a time all you have to think about is your feet on the path. In Bulawayo during the mission, I am running. I welcome the blur.

The next day came quickly. I was anxious, had I forgotten anything? James was at the office waiting for me when I arrived.

"Can I get a lift with you?" he said. "They told me you had a car."

"Sure. We have to go out early though."

He was wearing a light long-sleeve shirt with the sleeves rolled up. I noticed his strong, manly looking arms; the hair on his forearms was thick and dark.

Focus on what matters, I reminded myself.

On the drive out we talked about the schedule and the speakers. I was careful to keep the conversation focused on the mission, and to be honest, he was nice looking but there was nothing there, no electricity between us. I can usually tell if someone's interested in me, and he wasn't. Clearly. Which was a good thing.

"So where are you heading after the mission?" I asked, filling in time. "Back home to Australia?"

"No, I've got a round-the-world ticket. I'll go and see a friend in the UK, then to the States to see family for Christmas."

"Oh, nice. Well if you're up in Canada, drop in sometime!"

"No," he said flatly, dismissing me. "I can't imagine I'd ever go up there, just to Washington, DC."

Ouch. I changed the subject.

The hall was full that night. Stephen Lungu was speaking; there were people backed up out the doors. James and I sat outside to make room for other people. A group of kids played near us, waiting for their parents, smiling shyly at us and giggling. From outside we could hear Stephen shouting, the crowd laughing.

Then they began to sing in the way that only African voices can sing the darkness out of the night. Even the ground trembled. The night air was warm, laced with the sound of crickets and the sweet smell of hard-wood night fires.

"Have you ever heard anything as beautiful as that?" he said, the sounds of the African night casting a kind of spell.

Afterward, when we'd packed up the chairs and locked the equipment away, we drove Stephen Lungu back into town with us and dropped him off.

"Do you have to go home?" James asked. "Or do you want to get an ice cream?"

I was ready for an ice cream. We parked in front of Eskies Ice Cream and went up to the window to order.

He was much taller than I was and looked down into my eyes when he asked what I wanted.

What do I want? He has the kindest eyes, I thought.

"Vanilla, thanks." Keeping it simple was the right thing to do.

The ice creams melted down our wrists in the warm evening air.

When I looked at my watch next, it was midnight.

"We'd better go," I said. "There's an early meeting."

"I'll walk from your place; I'm staying in town this week."

But even after I parked the car in front of my building, we had many threads of conversation to tie up, things we both wanted to say before we said goodnight. When I looked at my watch again, it was 3 a.m.

James walked me to the door and held it open for me.

"Goodnight," he said gently.

His eyes, I thought. His eyes are astonishingly kind.

26

If you find yourself, one day, leaning up against a tree in the forest—say, a Douglas Fir—you will be touching the busiest part of the tree, where the tree is growing. The color of the wood inside this busy place will be light and golden, flowing and sticky with sap and nutrients, bursting out new cells and branches while you sit. This is where the tree lives.

But inside this golden sapwood layer lies the darker heartwood, the core of the tree. This is the core that has been the tree since it first sprouted from the earth. This is the first wood; it's dense and dark and permanent. No matter how tall and thick the tree becomes, the first wood is always there. After many years the first wood dies, but remains there just the same, at the core, remarkably preserved for hundreds of years.

I cannot tell you how much courage it had taken for me to first walk away from the people I had known and loved at the church that had been a family to me. I had come from a place of "first wood" that had ordered the world for men and women long before I was born; from a place that believed the words of the Bible had fallen from the mouth of God himself; a place that functioned on belief and obedience to values that had belonged to my family and my church family. Leaving was hard; leaving meant choosing to be alone.

The day Divide Creek took me, sweeping me up in a current that was strong and unfamiliar, I swam as best I could to keep my head above the water in panicked movements to stop myself from going under. I would need to swim. I was not altogether sure what I was swimming from, but I would not go back.

So the morning after that first ice cream at Eskies with James, I woke up panicked. What had I done? So easily I had let my guard down, toying with Norma David's games, a husband to take care of me, to help me back to the boat, to wrap my life up in wedding paper and casserole dishes, crochet clubs and Bible studies.

It was no one's fault but my own; I knew that. The first wood in me was pulsing with longing, not far beneath the new growth that had begun. I would need to be more careful.

But in spite of my best intentions, I could not be careful. Two full days passed, both nearly identical to that first. Busy with events and meetings, driving speakers and helpers back and forth across town, I watched James from a distance, fascinated. At night, after we'd stacked the chairs and closed the hall, we would stop at Eskies and eat ice cream in the car until late, debating ideas until my brain got tired, and laughing until it hurt too much to laugh anymore.

When a stream makes its way through the forest, the water tumbling seaward, no matter how determined and intentional its course, its journey is alone. How I welcomed the sound of a stream running parallel, nearby, just over the rise, where the forest had opened up.

But at night, I lay in bed unable to sleep.

Not even for a moment.

It was Norma David who kept me awake. Not her exactly but a dreamy image of her, as if she was there in the room with me when I closed my eyes.

When God chooses a husband for you, it's nothing to laugh about.

I caught myself.

It was *exactly* what I'd been afraid of. I should get up now, I thought, and drive somewhere far away from myself.

And at the last moment, sleep would slip in, bringing me, for a few precious seconds, to a gentle place where the alarm clock was poised to hit me like a wrecking ball.

On the third day, James and I stopped in to my apartment for afternoon tea before the next event.

I was exhausted.

Elizabeth was there with her friend; they were busy cleaning.

"Hi," I called out to the kitchen. "We just stopped in for a cup of tea."

"Okay, my dear," she called back.

"I'll put the kettle on, you look so tired," James said.

I wasn't myself.

I could hear him in the kitchen with the women, introducing himself, chatting.

"No, no," I could hear him say, "I'll make the tea, don't get up. . . ." He stayed in the kitchen with Elizabeth and her friend until the kettle boiled. I could hear them visiting, chatting about the weather and about where he was from.

I closed my eyes and prayed for a moment of sleep.

"Are you all right?" he said, carrying in the tea.

"I'm just tired," I told him. "I haven't slept for days. Lots going through my mind."

When it was time to go, I took the empty teacups into the kitchen.

Elizabeth was there by the sink with her hands in the air praising God. When she looked up and saw me, she rushed to me and pressed my face in between her hands. She closed her eyes and lifted her face to the ceiling.

"I thank you, my Jesus, I thank you."

Tears were rolling down her cheeks.

"I thank you, my Lord." She was often full of passion but not like this. I had no idea what this was about.

I smiled at her, feeling my face still held tightly in her hands, squished like a child's cheeks.

Then she let my face go. And stepped back.

"I'm sorry, my dear, but now I know. Now I know how much my God loves me. Now I *know* it."

I smiled back at her, confused.

"For weeks now I have been praying for you, my precious dear. I am praying for God every day and every night for you, my dear daughter. Every day, my dear, to my Jesus, that he would bring you a wonderful man, a kind man, to take care of you, my dear. And now he has brought him! He is such a special man, my dear, he is a good and kind man, my dear, and oh, how I am thanking the Lord Jesus for him." I couldn't think of anything to say. What could I say to that?

After the evening was over, we both went home early.

"Are you okay?"

I could tell by the way James looked at me that I must have looked awful.

"I just need to sleep," I said.

I climbed into my bed slowly that night, carefully, trying to slip off to sleep in secret, without Norma David or my brother or James or anyone else in the room with me.

Thankfully, that night there was no one there but me.

But still, sleep avoided me, as if it was a slippery, silent creature pressing back against the edges the room, circling, but refusing to come near, as if it had been ordered to keep its distance.

I didn't close the curtains that night. I left them open to stare at the night sky, hoping to catch God's eye. A windstorm was brewing. Leaves flew past my window even though the apartment was six stories up. I got up and looked down at the street and out across the lights of the townships.

"Can't you see how tired I am?" I said quietly, but loud enough so God could hear. "Why are you so distant? Why aren't you paying attention?"

I could see God, there in the wind that bent the trees and broke off branches, somehow wild and unreachable, whipping around the building, rattling and shaking the glass so hard I thought it would break. "What's wrong with you?" I shouted.

The moon seemed to dangle on some small thread in the sky while the wind spun round and round it.

The night stood back to watch.

I stood up on my bed and opened the window; I pushed it as wide as it would go. Six stories below, the laundry yard was empty.

First I put one leg through and then the next.

Watch me, I thought.

I wasn't jumping, of course, but maybe I'd wanted it to look that way.

The wind howled.

"Hey!" I shouted. "Where are you?"

Nothing.

So I leaned forward.

"What is *wrong*?" I shouted into the night.

The moon was silent too.

Someone walked by on the street below and looked up, but kept walking quickly, minding his own business.

"What do you *want*?" I yelled into the night. I was just so tired. "Can't you see this is killing me? I have to sleep!"

I shook my fist. If I'd had a rock, I'd have thrown it.

I was delirious.

My legs hung like a rag dolls out the window.

"Help me!" I yelled. "What do you want?"

I waited.

When the fiery part of me had burned itself out, I knew God was there, listening.

"Please help me," I said. "I need you." My heart split open. "Please tell me what to do."

You wouldn't have believed it unless you'd been there yourself. I hardly did.

But the wind stopped, just like that.

In one-half a second, the howl was gone from the night, and there I was hanging out the window staring at the moon dangling there in a clear night sky. Not a breath of wind.

So I said it again, gently, "Just tell me what to do."

But I knew it as soon as I said it, as soon as the words came out of my mouth—I knew what this was about. Of *course* I knew what this was about.

"Is it *him*? Is that what you mean?"

Silence.

"Is she right?" I asked then, a bit louder. "Is Norma David right?"

Somehow I already knew.

I shook my head. "I'm sorry," I said. "That's not enough. That's just not going to be enough. Can't you see that couldn't *possibly* be enough? I need more than that—a lot more."

Look at me, I thought to myself, noticing then what a sight this was. Me hanging out a window six stories up in the middle of the night in Africa shouting at the sky!

I couldn't trust myself.

I don't even know his last name, I thought.

"I don't even know his last name!" I said then, reminding God how ridiculous this was.

What is wrong with me? I thought. I am shouting at the sky about someone I don't even know, in the middle of the night. This is exhaustion; this is what delirious people do.

"All right," I said, because I could think of nothing else to do. "We'll make a deal. "

Silence.

"Did you hear me?" I shouted.

It's a wonder Patty didn't wake up and call the police.

"I said I would make a deal."

God waited. I felt it.

I knew about these things, I knew how this worked. I knew about Gideon and the fleece. This was one of those biblical moments and I was entitled to a bit more in this case. Gideon, in the book of Judges, when he wanted to be sure, when he needed to know for sure it was God, he asked for proof. It was something about a fleece being laid out and left wet in the morning, something about dew or rain. I deserved at least that.

Perhaps Gideon didn't trust himself either.

I thought of it on the spot, right there hanging out my window. If I were going to agree to this, I would need proof—good proof.

Zimbabwe had been in drought for seven years and I knew that rain was a tall order.

So that's what I asked for.

Rain. From the sky.

I would need it to rain, as proof.

Before the end of the mission, before the ten days were up, it would need to rain. Then I would know that Norma David was right, that God had chosen James for me.

"Did you hear me?"

There was nothing more to think about. It was out of my hands. I climbed back in the window, slipped into bed, and slept a deep, luxurious sleep.

27

The next morning the phone rang early, while I was in the shower.
"The phone is for you," Patty called, banging on the door. "I think
it's your father calling from Canada." I wrapped a towel around me and
ran to the phone.

"Hello?"

"Hi, honey," he said.

"Dad, hi!"

Something was wrong.

"You're okay?" he said.

"Yes, I'm fine. What's wrong?"

"Jim's been in the hospital for a few days," he said. "He's home now
and seems to be doing better but he didn't want me to tell you. He was
afraid you'd come home, and he didn't want that."

Oh, God.

"What's the matter? What happened?"

"We don't really know; he's having seizures. The ambulance has had
to come for him a few times. They're doing tests."

Oh, God.

"What do the doctors think?"

"We don't really know anything yet, that's why we didn't call; we
didn't want to worry you."

161

I am cold. I am suddenly so cold.

"But he asks me if you've called every couple of days. I guess he just wants to know you're okay."

I try to send him thoughts with my brain across the world.

"Should I come home?" I had two months to go. Two long months.

"Not yet, we should see what the doctors say."

"When can I call him?"

"You could call when they're here for lunch tomorrow, but don't let on you know. We're all trying to keep things on an even keel here until we sort out what's going on."

I talk for a minute or two more, yes, busy, in the middle of the mission, I'll call when they're over for lunch, tell him I love him. Love you too.

When I hung up the phone, I went into my room and shut the door behind me. I leaned up against it until I could not hold myself up anymore. I slid down the smooth surface into a puddle on the floor and fell to pieces.

"You're pretty quiet," James said when we arrived back in town; the day at Nketa was finally over.

I wondered what I should say. I hadn't told him about Jimmy.

"I got a phone call yesterday from home, that's all. "

"Do they miss you?"

"I don't think so. They're busy trying not to get divorced," I said, laughing a little. It was meant to sound light-hearted but it didn't come out that way.

"But my brother misses me, I think."

I don't know why I said this to him; I knew better than to start this.

"How old is he?"

"He's older than me; he's twenty-six, but he has lots going on in his life so it makes it hard to be away."

Silence. He left the space in case I wanted to say more.

I didn't want to say more, not at all.

But then I found myself recklessly opening my mouth.

"He's just gone into the hospital for a few days."

Stop now, I scolded myself, stop now. But I couldn't; I kept talking.

"That's what my dad called to tell me this morning. That my brother just wanted to know I was okay."

I turned my face to the window because I was no longer in control of the things that were locked away inside; everything was starting to spill out. Dammit, not now.

"What's happened?"

"Oh no," I said out loud then, partly to James but mostly to myself, trying to pull myself back together. "You really don't want to know the story—it's a long one. And it's pretty crazy."

"It's early," he said, his eyes twinkling. "It's only midnight, we've got hours."

I stared at him for a minute, thinking.

If nothing else, he is my friend, I thought.

My friend.

"What *is* your last name?" I asked. "I don't even know your last name."

"Gordon," he said. "James Gordon."

I smiled to myself. *Gordon.*

James Gordon.

And for the first time in my life, I began to tell the whole story.

By 2 a.m. my eyes were puffy and red, and the floor of the car was littered with tissues.

"I'm sorry," I said, looking at my watch, then in the mirror. "Look at me!"

But honestly, I didn't care.

His eyes were gentle.

I blew my nose again and smiled up at him.

He is kind, I thought to myself.

"I don't know what to do anymore. I came here to figure this out, but I haven't managed that yet. I can't go home empty-handed, but what choice do I have? They offered me a job in South Africa next year. I'd been thinking about staying on, but my brother. . . ."

"I don't know," he said then. "I think you'll need to go home. I don't think you have a choice really."

I knew he was right. "I just don't know what else to do. I don't have anymore answers."

He shook his head. "I don't know."

"I should probably go in," I said.

"Yeah, gosh, it's late again." But he sat still, not making any moves to get out of the car. We sat in the quiet of the night.

"Could I kiss you goodnight?" he said softly.

No one had ever asked me that before.

"Sure," I said. "If you want to." I tried not to sound nervous.

He leaned over and kissed me gently on the lips. Afterward, my lips felt the way the soft tufts of a dandelion must feel when they are kissed by the breath of a boy walking home barefoot on a summer evening.

28

*E*ven in a good year, the countryside around Bulawayo holds its
breath all the way through September and October, as if it's div-
ing through fire. October is called Suicide Month in Zimbabwe. The
earth has grown so hot and dry that people give up; they stop believing
that November will ever come. In a good year, the rain might come in
November. In a bad year, when the country has suffered a seven-year-
long drought, people stop believing altogether.

At the time I said it, out my window to the sky, I hadn't realized the
odds I'd set against it in giving God a window of a few days in September,
in the middle of a drought, to come up with rain.

So it came as no surprise really that every single day during the mission was as clear and as hot and as dry as the day before. And every single
day, when the sun shone brilliant and bold and when I could no longer
quite remember how it felt that night to hang out my window and shake
my fist at the sky, I felt foolish about the midnight deal I'd made.

I would not be heartbroken—a little sad, perhaps, but not heartbroken. James was a good person, kind and handsome, but I wasn't in love
with him. How could I be? I'd only known him for a few short days. He
lived in Australia for heaven's sake; it couldn't be more difficult.

No, it had been a mistake to let myself carry on. I liked him a great
deal and I hoped he knew that. We would write occasionally, Christmas

cards and a few letters; he'd be gone in a few weeks, and it was time I figured out what was next for me. He was right. I had to go home.

I thought about Sister Mary Francis and the nuns I'd met during reading break at Regent. I'd been working on a paper on monasticism, studying the lives of young women who, in the early Christian Church, refused to be married, resisting becoming servants of the men who had claimed them, instead devoting themselves to a life of prayer and service to the kingdom of God. There was something satisfying about their stories, making my own aloneness seem trivial. At Regent I had wrapped myself in the passion of their journeys, as if by reading about them I could insert myself into their company.

It wasn't that I couldn't have pursued the men I'd met, like Peter, the tiny little man from my church history class, with round glasses and mean little eyes, a large vocabulary and an equally large ego; or Tom, the generously uncomplicated young man who worked in a garage and sent postcards to me with little jokes and Bible verses; or Nathan, whose companionable presence in my life had grown tiresome, his pretense of intellect turning out to be nothing more than the churning of some- one else's ideas. The most significant relationship I'd had was with Dan, whose family was a pillar of the Evangelical Free Church, but he had been a bridge to a life that I'd left behind.

During reading break I went to live in a convent. And not just any convent, it was a cloistered convent, but I had no idea what that meant at the time. The Poor Clares live in silence, never leaving the convent. This is what "cloistered" means. They can speak to each other at the assigned recreation time, but their lives are devoted to worship, meditation, and prayer.

Seven times a day, when the little bell rang, even throughout the night, the nuns would gather in the chapel to pray and to sing, then scurry back to bed or to reading or to work until the next bell. When a week had passed, I was used to the routine. Some of the women had been there for more than fifty years. Imagine that—fifty years of silence. I had a private room that was not within the regular quarters, but joined in the inner hallway to the chapel. I saw no one unless we were at chapel.

My meals would appear like magic through a secret trapdoor in the wall. I would turn around or look up from my book and there was a tray, having appeared as if out of thin air—suddenly, there in my room, a beautiful tray with simple food, artfully arranged on little plates, always with a fresh flower or a verse of Scripture written on a tiny piece of paper, silent and mysterious. I was surprised by how healing this was for me. I did not feel alone there.

I had asked Sister Mary Clare for permission to speak to any of the nuns who were willing to meet with me. I would use what I learned for my paper. I had appointments, wrote notes, and asked difficult questions. Eight of the sisters were willing. The stories I heard were sometimes passionless and ordinary, but sometimes miraculous. Mostly, the writer in me was interested in why they'd chosen this kind of life.

Sister Mary Clare had said the call to chastity and "marriage to God" is a special calling. It's not for everyone. And just the way she said it made it seem as if those who were called to it were special or sacred. Did I feel a twinge of jealousy? Perhaps I did.

"But why doesn't God call everyone to this life?" I asked her. "Why does he just choose some people?" It seemed clear to me that the longing for a companion with whom I could share my life was not going away. Did this mean I was not called, not chosen, not special?

"Everyone is called to something," she said. "The call to our life is special and wonderful, of course. It's not lonely here; in fact it's the opposite. How I long to be alone sometimes!" she laughed. "But the call to a marriage designed by God is also a special calling."

She was trying to convince me.

Sister Mary Francis was next. She had things to say, but she was guarded.

I pushed further.

"So what I'm wondering is, if you think that God calls us—you specifically—to a life dedicated *only* to Him? What I mean is, do you think that becoming a nun, the spouse of Christ, in a sense . . ."

"Oh, it's not in a sense, it's very real," she interrupted.

"Yes, of course," I said, sorry I'd seemed dismissive. "What I mean is, do you think that in joining a religious order and vowing to live your life in service to God alone, you find your ultimate happiness?"

I think what I was looking for that day was a simple *yes*.

Sister Mary Francis thought for a while and didn't answer at first. She was the fifth of the sisters I'd interviewed that day, but I felt she was being more open with me than the others had been:

"Of course this life is very definitely a calling for many of us. But it can also be an escape for some. Sometimes people end up here, in this life, because their hearts have been broken, or because they don't seem to fit anywhere else, or because they wanted to do the right thing and weren't sure what else to do. God honors these women, welcoming them, making them his own." I wrote notes as she talked, hoping not to interrupt the way she seemed to be letting herself speak freely.

"But there are other callings that have nothing to do with poverty and chastity, that I believe offer as many challenges and opportunities for service and growth . . . and for love." She stopped and reached for a sip of tea from the mug on her lap.

"I think we miss the importance of this kind of a calling. The calling to take up the covenant of marriage—the sacred experience of the Trinity reflected in husband, wife, and Holy Spirit—is not to be dismissed as somehow less than the call to a religious order. In fact, in many ways, it might be more challenging, more difficult to get right, and yet taken less seriously by so many in contemporary society."

She relaxed a little.

"I've seen only a few marriages like this. They are marriages put together by God, and they are powerful; they are evidence of the Holy Spirit at work in the world."

She put her mug on the table.

"I was in love with a good man once," she confided, leaning forward. "And he with me." She sighed deeply, as if she was seeing him in front of her eyes. "But my family insisted I choose the Church," she said. "I tried to do the right thing. That was thirty-six years ago. I've been here ever since."

"But do you regret it?" I asked, certain she'd say she didn't.

She smiled softly, looking deep in my eyes. "Yes," she said, "sometimes I do."

29

$\mathcal{I}$'d forgiven myself by Sunday for the way I'd let myself carry on inside. It was the final day of the mission, the culmination of weeks of work, and I wanted to enjoy it. I didn't want to be down on myself. Deep down I knew I wasn't beyond hope—a bit crazy, but not beyond hope; I hoped I'd learn something from this.

Just for fun, I checked the sky when I woke up. I pushed open the window and stared up at the sun.

"Good morning!" I called out the window and smiled, making my peace in a way that only the sky would understand. I went to church in town with Sheckie and Douglas, had lunch with Reuben afterward, and then came home to change. The final rally was at 3 p.m. It would be held in a huge football oval with the capacity to hold the thousands of people who were coming.

James knocked on my door early; I'd promised him a ride out to the rally.

"Come in, I'm still getting ready."

"It's okay—I brought a newspaper."

He put the kettle on.

I'll miss this, I thought. He'll go back out to the farm and then off to another camp before he flies away to the other side of the world. It's funny how close you can feel to someone in your mind, in the private world inside your head. When I looked up at his face and noticed he'd forgotten to shave, I felt as if I could reach out and touch his skin, and it would be the most natural thing to do, as if it had been that way forever.

I will never forget the way he said it, then, the way his voice sounded, hushed. But the words themselves hit my ears like a train:

"There's a cloud in the sky," he said.

I was sure I'd misheard him.

"Come and look at this! There's a *cloud* in the sky."

I went out to the lounge room.

He was standing on the balcony staring up at the sky.

He was right. Here was an honest-to-God cloud in the sky, a genuine puffy white cloud with a grey belly that looked like it did not belong in that brilliant blue sky.

It was a cloud.

"That's a cloud!" I said to him, turning to look at him, a thousand thoughts flooding my mind.

"I know," he said. "That's what I said."

It was right there, out of place in a bright blue sky. It was not a big cloud, not a rain cloud, but it was a cloud nonetheless.

I went back to finish getting ready.

In a few minutes we were in the car, and as I was reversing out of my parking spot, I thought I saw a drop of water on the back window, which was ridiculous, of course. I was imagining it.

As I pulled out to cross the intersection, a drop of water landed on my windshield. This time there was no mistaking it. It was a real drop of water. I put the brakes on and stared at it there on the glass. It was real.

I kept driving; my brain was reeling. What exactly was *rain*? Was it a drop? Was it *one* drop of water? Was that supposed to count as *rain*? Surely that couldn't count as rain.

It wasn't rain—it was a drip.

What counted as rain, for heaven's sake? I should have been more specific.

Then there were five and six drops on my windshield. Then four more. Cars were pulling off the road everywhere, with drivers abandoning their cars, leaving their doors wide open, standing in the middle of road with their hands open to the sky in utter disbelief.

The red dry earth was splotched with occasional dark patches, like footprints of something mysterious passing by. I did not pull over; I was having trouble concentrating. I knew I'd better keep moving, keep the car crawling while the street was empty; I was peering over the steering wheel, having a hard time breathing.

Was this rain? What *was* it, if not rain?

I have no idea what James was doing; I completely forgot he was in the car with me. Like everyone else on the street, I was completely and utterly struck by this strange appearance of the cloud, but unlike everyone else on the street, it shook everything inside of me down to my deepest core.

✻

I parked the car at the edge of the field. Thousands of smiling black faces and dancing bodies filled the green grassy bowl. And they were singing. The afternoon was filled with a harmony you might only ever hear again in heaven, the drums beating out the path for my feet to follow, a city of hands clapping together, shouting out to the Lord, voices spiraling like birds in flight, weaving through the air.

When the crowd began to sing the next song, I felt a rumbling in the air.

Do you understand this?

It was a rumbling like an earthquake in the air. I couldn't hear it above the voices, but I felt it. There was something coming. The voices were singing out to heaven:

What a mighty God we serve.
What a mighty God we serve.

And somehow, like a fist on a drum that had been waiting, waiting for this moment, the thunder cracked open the sky. The heavens poured.

Buckets of water poured from the sky, rain falling heavier than I knew was possible, falling like a waterfall.

People ran for the trees, laughing, but I didn't run.

I looked up at the sky.

My God, it's raining.

It's raining!

I felt my body move without me, into the field of people dancing; I was crying and laughing, but no one knew the difference; the water was everywhere, absolutely everywhere.

We stood at the front by the choir while the whole field of people sang and praised God for this rain. My feet found the rhythm of the drums and when I glanced up, there he was: James, laughing and dancing in the rain beside me.

He has no idea what's just happened, I thought. But it didn't matter right then.

I lifted my face to the sky and let the water wash over me, the heavenly African rain falling like a promise. There he is, I thought. There is my husband, my friend, the man I will spend my life with.

There is James.

Afterward, when the field had emptied and the day was complete, we were both quiet, thoughtful. It didn't matter what next. If God could pull off rain like that, I didn't need to worry about what next.

We drove home in a soft, exhausted silence.

"Do you mind if I come up for awhile?" James asked. "I think we should talk."

"Sure," I said. "Let's have tea."

He didn't say anything for a long time; I could see he was thinking.

"Are you okay?" I asked him.

"Yes, I just don't know where to start."

"What do you mean?" I said, distracted by my own thoughts.

"We've got a lot to talk about."

Yes, I thought, you don't know the half of it.

He took a breath.

"Can you come and sit on the couch beside me?" He put his hand on my knee for a minute then changed his mind. "So I've been thinking, lately, about you and about me."

My heart started to pound.

"I know how this sounds—it's crazy and it won't make any sense but bear with me."

I waited, letting him slow his thoughts down enough to speak.

"I don't even know how to say this, so I'll just say it."

He swallowed and nodded his head, as if he was talking himself through this.

Now, you might think the rain that afternoon was unbelievable, but the real miracle was coming.

"I'd said to God," he stammered, "that if it rained before the end of the mission, I would ask you to marry me." *Marry me.*

And then I couldn't hear anything but my breath, because it was impossible.

It was impossible to even imagine.

He was nervous, shifting in his seat, sweat on his forehead.

"I know how crazy that sounds—*of course I know*—but you have to know, the rain was . . . this is too hard . . ."

I reached for his knee and squeezed.

"It's okay," I said. "I know. I already know."

And then I told him. I told him about Norma David and the window and the sky and the wind. We didn't even have words for what it meant. We didn't cry or laugh or smile. It was too strange for any kind of feeling to exist in the space with us.

"But what does this all mean?" he said.

"I don't know," I said.

We didn't kiss or celebrate or fall into each other's arms. That's what happens in movies; this was real life—this was the rest of our lives we were talking about. This was not a movie. This was real. We needed some sleep, some distance.

"I'll call you tomorrow," he smiled, but it was a forced, worried smile. "Goodnight."

"Goodnight," I said and closed the door.

Four days later, we sat in the car outside the farm. He was leaving in the morning. I looked over at the silhouette of his face as the sun set, a red ball in the sky slipping away quickly.

"Heather," he said carefully. "Will you marry me?"

The words came out of my mouth easily, as if they had always been there.

"Yes," I said. "I will marry you."

In three months time I would marry a man I hardly knew.

30

On a sunny February afternoon at the Evangelical Free Church in Prince George, I married James Gordon. You can imagine the astonished faces when I asked to book the church. He arrived in Canada in a snowstorm a few days before Christmas; we'd all been waiting. I hadn't seen him for a month; I worried I wouldn't recognize him. I had one creased picture of him with a group of friends in Nketa. I could hardly remember him.

It was a small and simple wedding put together on a few hundred dollars. James's family flew out from Australia, anxious to meet the new bride, understandably wary, I could see. Who could blame them?

Even by the time of our wedding we hardly knew each other. We'd spent most of our time trying to hold together the shreds of my family.

When I'd arrived home from Zimbabwe, just six months had passed, but Jim was different; it was as if he was absent from his body, vacant. He seemed to have disappeared and left the carcass of himself behind. His neck and face were oddly swollen, and he held his head stiffly and tilted, gripping the backs of chairs or doorframes for support. His eyes were no longer shiny and searching—now they were nothing but glass, like eyes inserted by a taxidermist, as if he didn't see anything. He gave me an awkward hug when I saw him at the airport, working hard to lift his arms and squeeze.

"The doctors say they can't find anything wrong with him," my dad said.

I am careful when I write about this time. I'd been away; I hadn't faced what had happened during those months. I cannot imagine how difficult it must have been for the people who had loved him through those long days.

"He just lies in his bed crying for days and days! He won't stop," my mother said, exasperated. She was tired, preoccupied with what she had to organize. She was, at last, making plans to leave. It was time. We were both grown children; there was no need to keep pretending. The wedding was a surprise she hadn't counted on. It was a delay she found difficult.

Jim's wife had given up too.

"I have to go to work; I can't help him," she'd said. "He starts crying from the minute he wakes up! It's ridiculous! Get up and get going, I tell him, but he doesn't listen."

I've never heard good science about this, but I believe it's possible for people to develop a kind of black hole in their heart. That black hole absorbs things, swallows them whole, and nothing can escape, not love and not worry. It's not common, but it happens, I think, when the conditions have been difficult and damaging. This must have been what had happened while I was away. The people who were meant to care for Jimmy could not. Their hearts had trapped inside the love they would have needed to help him. They were no longer able to care for him the way he needed them to.

When James arrived, Jimmy and Uta had a small party, a few people to their house for snacks and drinks. It was Boxing Day. The crowd of Christmas visitors was leaning against the counter in their kitchen, others were piled up on couches and cushions in their living room, chatting, eating snacks, drinking German beer or glasses of wine; glasses clinked and people toasted the festive season.

Fireflies 177

And there was Jimmy—standing in the corner of the kitchen, surrounded by people but somehow completely alone, talking to the corners
of the ceiling, whispering into the air beside him, pressing his fingertips
together in front of his chest, like a scene from a movie. I stopped following the conversation I'd been part of and stared.

James noticed too.

I made my way across the room to him.

"Who are you talking to?" I asked him.

"To the creatures," he said. "They usually stay on the edge of my easel
but they're out here tonight. They should go back."

"Oh," I said. "Are they still in here?"

"Of course they are. Look there's one."

He pointed.

"See? They go straight back into my art room when I notice them.
But they're all over the ceiling in here tonight." He explained them to me,
where they lived and what they did. He was surprised I couldn't see them.

"Come into my art room and I'll show you what I'm doing," he said.

I'm scared again. I'd forgotten what it felt like.

"Jimmy, how long have you had these creatures?"

"Oh, a long time. They've always been there, I just didn't let them
out here."

Later that night I asked his wife about it.

"Oh my goodness, Uta, how long has this been going on?" I am so
deeply sorry, then, that I haven't been here to help her through all of this.
How has she coped alone, working through this without much support?

"What do you mean?" she said.

"How long has Jimmy been seeing the creatures?"

"What? That's weird!"

"Did you know he sees creatures?"

"No! Don't, you're scaring me!"

"So you don't know about any creatures?"

"Stop it!"

She walked away.

By the time of our wedding, I'd begun to wonder if having Jimmy as a groomsman was a good idea. Mostly I tried not to look at him, wobbling inside between empathy and anger. I knew he was drinking, but I didn't know how much. I didn't know he'd pried open the cellar of their little house to stash the bottles down there. No one knew. And I didn't know the pile of bottles in the basement would fill a dump truck. When I looked at him, my heart felt like someone had taken it in their hands, wringing the life from it, the way you might twist a small creature's neck to snap it.

Somehow we got through it. A kind woman from church offered to "do the flowers" for us. I didn't realize at the time she meant arranging plastic flowers from the bin in the basement of the Bay into tidy plastic bouquets, but what did it matter? My mother was annoyed that I wouldn't wear stockings and my mother-in-law couldn't imagine a bride without a veil; I wasn't bothering with either. I couldn't care less about decorations or veils.

When James's mother asked me to choose a china pattern, I froze, having no idea what to tell her, wanting only to run screaming away from it all. Instead I smiled and told her I'd give it some thought. At home I fell in a heap of tears trying to explain to the man who would soon be my husband why his mother's very generous offer had turned me into a weeping wreck. I did not want china or casserole dishes or place settings.

We were married on February 29, 1992. It was the warmest February day I could remember. Snow that had fallen that week was melted by midmorning on our wedding day. We didn't have a photographer, but we had a friend with a camera, so we drove around in a collection of cars in search of an appropriate setting for photos.

The park near the church was already green on the edges where the snow had melted. I lifted my dress to step through the puddles, and the cluster of wedding attendants gathered on the grass, laughing comfortably now that the formal part was over.

The snowbanks stood back. I balanced on my toes to avoid my heels sinking into the wet earth. At my feet I noticed a small patch of clover that had survived the winter. I wanted to bend to the ground and search the leaves on my knees, but who would have understood what it meant, that day, for the bride to find a patch of clover on her wedding day?

"Smile," called the people with cameras flashing.

I reached for James's hand.

Jimmy had given us a beautiful drawing he'd had framed. In the drawing there is a baby elephant in the foreground and the face of an adult elephant softly sketched in behind.

"It's kind of like the adult elephant remembering," he'd said that day, pointing out it meant something more, but there was noise in the room and I couldn't hear him very well, people were crinkling paper and pouring coffee and talking to me from across the room.

What I wouldn't give to sit with him now and ask him about that drawing. All these years later, when I stare at the drawing, I can see now that it is not about the baby elephant.

The drawing is about the eye of the adult elephant: the eye is tired, weary, worn-out from the journey.

The eye has seen enough.

The eye is finished.

Why didn't I see that then?

When it was all over, we drove our rental car to the room we'd booked for our wedding night at the Holiday Inn on George Street. It was a plain room, clean and simple. I looked out the window and saw someone who looked like Charlie crossing the street. He was not, of course, wearing the turquoise jacket. Was it Charlie? I closed the curtains.

We were both tired, ready to fly out to Australia the next day so James could collect his things. We'd decided to start our life in Canada first, to help my family.

And there we were, on our wedding night.

I'd never slept with James, or anyone else for that matter. I'd "saved myself" for my husband. But what does that mean really, to have saved oneself for marriage? I wondered.

Was I about to lose myself now? What had that meant all these years?

He'd never been kinder to me than he was that night. Comforting me, knowing what this meant. He wrapped his arms around me and kissed the back of my neck.

"We don't have to do this tonight," he said. "If this all feels like too much for one day."

"No," I said. "I want to."

And I did—I'd never wanted anything more clearly in my life.

We were given to each other that night, in the Holiday Inn on George Street.

For this reason a man shall leave his father and mother and be joined to his wife and the two shall become one flesh. For this reason the hills will gather the tumbling streams, and the two will become one. For this reason the forest will open wide, the hills will rise up to cradle them, and the sun and the moon and the stars will light their way.

Yes, for *this*, I saved myself.

Together, we were a river.

31

As I write this, a mysterious underground fire burns 40 kilometers from Eagle, Alaska. No one knows exactly what's burning, but it's been burning underground for more than a year. An underground fire in Centralia, Pennsylvania, has been burning since 1962. No one knows how many hundreds of underground fires burn across the world, arising spontaneously or ignited by lighting, but once a fire takes hold of a fuel source underground, it can burn for hundreds of years.

When we were young, Jimmy was careless with the fire that burned inside of him; he sat alone beside it, drinking heavily, stoking the flames, stacking it high with whatever he could find while the flames grew.

I hadn't seen the flames for some time; I could still smell a lingering smoke but I dismissed it.

We'd been home from Australia for three weeks when I started to notice rage flashing across his face, a fury that he could not contain.

"Sorry, sorry," he'd say then, but he was not sorry for being angry, he was sorry that he'd let it be seen.

He confided in me then.

He told me one afternoon that he felt he was dangerous, that he was scared of himself.

"In what way?" I asked him, trying to understand.

"In no way, never mind." He was coming up from the basement of our parents' house where he still had his studio. He was standing on the stairs, holding on to the railing, catching me on my way out the door.

Wasn't that always the way? Why was I always on my way out the door?

That was when he told me openly, for the first time, about Mr. Diakiw.

"Do you know what it's like remembering now?" he said. "It's done terrible things to my brain. You don't know what it's like to live inside my head. I can't get away from it."

There are things I can't write here, things you don't need to know. What you need to know is that the images stayed inside of him, but not just the images. I believe he'd taken those images and fueled them, constructing a world he could not escape.

"Do you know what it's doing in my brain? Do you know my thoughts are eating me from the inside out?"

The demons, he tells me, won't let it go, none of it.

I almost cannot bear to write this, to put to paper my total failure to take the right steps, to call a different doctor or the police or the prime minister or the pope—somebody. I went through it all in my mind that day. He'd been to see several doctors and psychiatrists; he'd tried medications.

In the end they said there was nothing wrong with him.

He drank too much. That was it.

I had no idea what to suggest. I just looked at him and told him I needed to think about it.

That night James and I talked about it for hours.

"We should at least try," I said.

At least we could do that—we had to at least try, for God's sake! Otherwise what had it all been for?

"I'll ask him," I said, and I picked up the phone. I explained to Jimmy what we were thinking.

"Can we pray over you?" I said. The words in my mouth felt wooden and scripted, inauthentic, dispassionate. I was embarrassed. But it was worth being embarrassed about. It was the last thing left. How could we not at least *try*?

"Sure. I don't care," he said. He was up for it, like agreeing to try a new soft drink.

He sounded almost relieved. Of course he was relieved; that was what I'd gone to Africa for, that was what Regent had been about, but so far I hadn't delivered.

"We'll come over tomorrow."

※

When we arrived the next day, he was there, the same as he'd been for weeks.

"Wanna beer?" he said, only partly joking. Then, "So . . . where do you wanna do this thing?" He was a bit nervous, cracking jokes.

"Are you okay with this?" I asked. This was it; my one shot at it. This is what I went to learn. All I wanted to do was leave, actually. I was embarrassed. Maybe I should have accepted that beer. But there was only one reason I was there.

"Go ahead," he said, holding his arms wide. Was he smirking?

Could I run for the door?

I looked at James; he shrugged. I felt small and pathetic.

"Well, why don't we sit on the couch?" I really said it that way, as if I was some kind of therapist.

Jimmy sat in the middle and James and I on either side of him. We put our hands on his back to pray.

"God, we bring Jimmy before you; we hold his life out to you in Jesus's name," I said.

James began to pray in tongues, softly whispering.

Jimmy was sitting between us, calmly. No reaction.

I muttered a few more lines that sounded hollow.

But then I felt something, as if I'd seen it in the corner of my eye, but it was not visual, it was something I could feel, thin and slippery. Darkness.

I took a breath and spoke directly to it, hiding there on the edge.

"In the name of Jesus," I began, summoning the darkness to pay attention. When I do this, Jim's whole back suddenly stiffens as if a rod has been shoved up his spine.

My hand feels strange.

He closes his eyes and his head drops back behind him, his body stiff and arched.

We keep praying.

The air in the room was suddenly hazy. Was it really?

I looked for James, who was less than two feet from me on the other end of the couch, but I could hardly see him in the thick air.

The words came naturally, somehow, spilling out of my mouth, flowing fast without me even thinking. But they were not Michael Green's words; they were words that came from somewhere inside of me, as if they'd been waiting a long time for this fight.

I was not afraid anymore; I had nothing left to lose.

The words on my tongue were from an angry place, all those years frightened to death, sneaking past it up the stairs to my room; I would not be afraid anymore—never again. I prayed with my voice reaching, straining to find a way; my arm on my brother's back felt heavy.

I am tired.

I am suddenly so tired.

His body was shaking, his back stiff as a plank.

"Keep going!" I heard someone whisper from across the room. "You've got to keep going."

Was someone else there in the room with us? The haze was so heavy I couldn't see. It was a man's voice. When he stepped closer and I could see: it was Grandpa Young, a cigarette in the corner of his mouth; he was old—too old to fight—but his fists were up.

"You leave that boy alone you black-hearted son of a bitch!" he shouted.

Then we were back at Stuart Mackenzie's party; it was my brother and me.

"Fight, fight, fight!" I heard them shouting.

"Get out of the way!" I screamed.

I see my brother on the ground; his face being hammered into the dirt.

He was holding his groin, covering his face. People stood watching, doing nothing. I clawed my way into the middle and grabbed on with both hands. I feel skin under my fingernails.

"Get off him!" I scream.

Jim is lying there in the dirt, not moving.

The crowd disappears.

"Jimmy."

I touch his cheek.

I feel his blood with my fingertips, warm and slippery on his face, in his hair.

"Jimmy. Can you hear me?"

I rub his back with my hand.

"It's okay, you'll be okay."

I am too small to lift him.

I'm just too small.

"My glasses," he says.

On my knees, in dirt and leaves, I search with my hands, moving across the ground, sweeping the driveway with my fingertips for answers, calling back to him. "It's okay, you'll be okay."

※

Then we were not at Stuart Mackenzie's party. We were on a couch in a living room. His body was shaking, his neck muscles bulging like I'd seen years before, as if something was inside his skin.

James was praying louder now; I could hear his words like drums, calling us on. The bulging neck tightened, his body arched sharply backward, as if something was reaching up from inside of him to climb from his throat. I shouted from deep in my lungs, "Leave him, in Jesus's name."

At that he fell forward in a slump, crying, whimpering, hanging like a rag doll.

"Don't stop," he wept. "Help me, please."

I wanted to lift his face to mine, to press my cheek against his.

"Keep praying, keep praying, there's more . . ." he said.

So we prayed.

"I am speaking to you, Darkness—you have no right to be here!"

His eyes were closed, his body limp. Then I didn't quite understand what I heard at first. He was humming. What was that song?

He was singing and crying, in a small boy's voice, no louder than a whisper,

"Jesus loves me this I know. . . ." Great sobs crept up his throat and spilled out. "Little ones to him belong, we are weak but he is strong. . . ."

He was singing it like a promise, like it was the only thing that mattered.

I could see him, then, running down the aisle at Ness Lake Bible Camp.

I could see the fireflies filling up my jar.

"Keep praying—there's more." He didn't open his eyes.

So we prayed, shouting at whatever it was, in Jesus's name, commanding, praying, rebuking.

But we all felt it.

Whatever it was, it was not budging, not even a bit; it wasn't going anywhere.

And we knew it.

I couldn't shout any louder; I couldn't grab anything or touch anything. I couldn't even get near it, whatever it was; that much I knew.

I am too small, I thought. *I am still too small.*

He sat up then, abruptly, and rested back against the cushions.

At first I thought he was crying, but he wasn't.

In fact he was laughing. Or someone was laughing.

He fell onto the floor then and rolled around with his legs in the air, laughing and laughing.

But it wasn't his laugh. It was strange.

"You're just children," said a voice coming from his mouth. "What do *you* know?" The voice was snide, malicious, evil.

"Look at you!" the voice said. "You're just children!"

He spat the words out, disgusted.

I felt like a child.

"You want to see everything we've got in here?"

I noticed the "we."

I breathed carefully.

"I'm not scared of you," I said to the voice, less sure now.

The voice laughed.

"Yes, you are," the voice said. "You're terrified."

And I was.

At that moment I heard the front door open and slam shut.

Uta came into the living room.

Jim was lying on the floor in front of us.

"What are you *doing*?" she shouted at him.

She couldn't stand the sight of him.

"Uh oh . . ." said the voice, like a cartoon character, mocking her.

At that, she marched across the living room, wound up and kicked him in the stomach; then she stormed out of the house.

He lay on the floor groaning, swearing, holding his stomach.

It was over.

"I think you'd better go now," he said.

"Are you all right?"

"Fuck," he said, shaking his head.

32

The next week, when our mother left for the other side of the country, Jimmy decided to move home so Dad wasn't alone.

"I need a favor," he said. "I need you to help me quit drinking."

James and I looked at each other.

"What do you want us to do?"

"Just stay with me when Dad's not here. Don't let me out of your sight for a week or two."

"Jim, I have to go to work."

I'd just started a new job; I knew I couldn't stay with him.

"I can stay with you," James said. His work permit hadn't come through yet; he had time.

I honestly don't know how James coped with us all in those early days; he must have felt as if he'd been swallowed by insanity. I remembered the words from Hebrews, *Come boldly and you will find help for what you need.* I remembered feeling so certain that it was not me who needed anything. How little I knew about what I would need, then; what my family would need. I didn't know his name would be James, that he would step bravely into our lives and help to carry the load.

So the first thing we did was empty the hiding spots.

"Let's go through it all," my brother said, without hesitation. He was determined; this was serious. We pulled bottles out of the backs of cupboards, from under desks and from in the garage. "You'll need to take my keys too."

So I did.

"Promise me, no matter what I say, you won't let me out of this."

So for the next ten days, James arrived every day at eight o'clock and stayed all day. Jimmy painted, watched television, made lunch. James read the newspaper, worked on his résumé, made the best of it.

Jimmy seemed okay.

But by Saturday morning of the second weekend, he asked for his keys back.

"Hey, I need my keys, I've got to pick up some stuff from my house."

"What stuff?" I said. "I'll drive you."

He looked at me like I was crazy.

"Just give me my keys, I'll be back in half an hour."

"I can drive you, I don't mind. Jim, it's better if I . . ."

"Give me my fucking keys!"

Rage.

"Jim . . ."

"Give me my keys!" He hit the wall with his fist and the paintings shook. "Just fucking give me my keys." He spoke quietly now, deliberately, threatening me with his eyes.

So I went to the place I'd hidden them in my room upstairs and threw them down at him. I hoped they'd hit him on the head.

"Thank you," he said with a fake smile. "I'll be back in half an hour. I just have to get my toothbrush and things. I don't need a babysitter."

I ignored him.

Later that day he told James he would no longer need him to come over.

"I'm okay now," he said. "You don't need to come anymore."

"I don't mind," James said. "I can come."

"No—I don't need you here." But what he meant was, stay out.

The next week James started a temporary job at Canadian Tire stacking boxes in the warehouse while he looked for work. He was a chemical engineer; he was bound to find work in a pulp and paper town like Prince George. In the meantime, our friends Tom and Linda Steadman, who owned Canadian Tire, found him enough to do. They were good people who had been like parents to me. I have known my whole life that I could count on them.

It was May, the air was warm, and the robins had arrived in town again. Jimmy was trying hard to be happy, I could see. For the first time in weeks, he was chatty, joking around. He made dinner for us one night. The world felt softer.

Was it real?

James and I were twenty-four years old, living in a basement suite near Fort George Park without much money to live on. We'd been married for eight weeks, but our life together was only ours when my dad or my brother didn't need us, which was almost never. We brought dinner over to my dad's during the week, or the four of us went out together to a restaurant. We watched movies with them on weekends, sat together on the back deck looking out over the valley, listening to the birds in the trees and hoping we were through the worst of it. It felt like we'd survived some terrible storm. Jimmy and my dad had set up their new lives together, both of them surviving.

❦

One Sunday we were barbequing on the back deck.

"Look," Jimmy said to me, holding up my old Polaroid camera. "Look what I found in the basement."

"Hey! I got that for Christmas when I was eleven; where'd you find it?"

"Smile!" he said and took a photo of me making a crazy face. When the picture developed he held it out to me. "Hang on to this picture, you'll want to remember this day."

"Why?" I said, not paying attention to anything but the warm sun on my back, the easiness of the evening, the smell of the steaks cooking on the barbeque.

"Why today?"

"No reason, you'll just want to remember what a good day it was; you know, how happy we are."

It was an odd thing to say. I put the picture in my pocket because it seemed to matter to him.

"I'm going out of town tomorrow," my dad said at dinner. "I've been telling Jimmy to come with me, but he says he doesn't want to." He was looking for support, someone to encourage Jim to go with him.

"I don't need a babysitter, I'm twenty-six years old for God's sake."

"I know, I just worry." My dad looked tired.

"These guys will probably come over anyway, don't worry." Jimmy looked at us.

"Sure, we'll come over," I said. I looked over at James and wondered how much more of this he could take. He looked tired too.

"Don't worry, I'll be fine," Jim said.

When we left that night, I hugged my dad.

"He's an adult, Dad. You can't chain him up."

"Okay, you guys are coming over tomorrow night, right?" Jimmy called up from the basement. Why was he so insistent?

"Yeah, we'll drop by after dinner," I said.

"For sure, eh? Just come over."

He went back downstairs and called out behind him, "Don't forget."

James and I didn't talk much on the way home. What was there to say? We didn't really have anything to say to each other. Everything we did revolved around my brother and my dad. Our entire history together had been about looking after them.

We still hardly knew each other.

"Are you okay?" I said on our way to sleep.

"I'm good."

But his voice was empty; he answered in a way that drew a curtain between us before we went to sleep. This was not a marriage; this was a home-care arrangement for my family. Something had to change.

I was tired at work the next day. The weekends were hard. There was so much extra family time to fill in. It was 10:30 in the morning when I closed the door to my office and sat quietly drinking a cup of coffee. I had a window that looked out from the third floor across Victoria Avenue to the strip mall across the street and the downtown liquor store. I watched people come and go, people staggering up from George Street to wait outside the liquor store, hoping to catch a handout whenever the door opened.

When I looked up from my coffee, I was pretty sure I saw someone who looked like my brother walk through the parking lot and go into the liquor store.

I was seeing things, I told myself, since Jim had quit drinking. Still I paid attention, kept my eyes steady on the door, just in case. I only had to watch for a minute or two. He was quick. I was not seeing things.

There was my brother with a large bottle-shaped brown bag in his hand, gripping the neck of it as he strode across the parking lot to my dad's car. If I could have thrown my desk out the window at him, I would have that morning. If there'd been a door to run out of, I would have chased him and smashed in the windows.

I hated him.

I couldn't stand this anymore.

After work that day I didn't talk until long after we got home to our basement suite.

"I hate him," I said then as if out of nowhere, me stirring the pasta, tears running down my face. "I hate him, James. . . ."

He turned off the stove and pulled me to the couch and hugged me. "Shhh . . ." he said.

When I started to cry, I didn't stop for hours.

I sobbed and sobbed as I had never sobbed in my whole life; I could not stop. We climbed into bed and James pulled the covers up to our necks and held me.

"I can't do this anymore," I said.

I could see it was starting to get dark.

"We're supposed to go over there," I said, finally, dreading it. When I sat up and saw my swollen face in the mirror, my red eyes, my matted hair, I changed my mind. "I'll call him and tell him we can't come."

It took all my strength just to get out of bed and go to the phone.

It rang twenty times and no answer.

"He's not even home!"

He didn't care half as much as I did. I spent so much of myself worrying, helping, fixing, and he just didn't care.

It was killing me.

It was killing us all.

"And he's got my dad's car! I just hope he doesn't smash it up. That's all my dad needs right now."

I washed my face and put on my pajamas. We left the soggy spaghetti in the pot and ate potato chips and Oreo cookies instead. I dialed the phone once more and let it ring; still no answer.

James was already asleep by the time I climbed into bed.

Something had to change.

By the next morning, I was rested. I had no more tears left. In many ways, the first hours of that day were exactly as any other. We showered, had breakfast, and I dropped James at work at Canadian Tire. I parked my car in the pay parking lot near my office and walked in slowly through the back glass door. I pushed "3" on the elevator and smiled at Yvonne at the front desk when I walked into the office. I closed the door behind me.

I didn't turn my computer on that morning. Instead I picked up the phone and dialed Jimmy again. It was 9 in the morning. I wanted to ask where he'd been, make sure the car was okay. But there was no answer.

That was the first time I thought something might be wrong.

I dialed the phone again and let it ring, for a long time.

When there was no answer, I picked up my purse.

"I'll be out for awhile," I said to Yvonne at the front.

"That was a quick morning," she said.

"I've got something I have to do, but I won't be long."

I drove up the highway from town to the Hart, looking down dirt roads and in the ditches hoping to catch sight of my father's car, abandoned somewhere. When I passed the Hart Wheel Inn, I slowed down. He sometimes went there. Maybe he'd gone for breakfast, I'd thought, but my dad's car wasn't there.

My heart thudded hard inside my chest when I saw tow truck lights flashing and a police car parked on the edge of the road near the swamp. I shivered. Oh, God. But they were stopped talking to a man in a pickup, not to my brother.

By the time I pulled into the driveway, I was worried. The front door was locked so I used my key. The house was quiet.

"Jim?" I called. "Jim! You here?"

No answer.

I went to the garage to see if the car was there.

It was.

The car was there. What did that mean?

And so were his shoes. His shoes were there too.

He had to be here.

What did that mean?

I walked into the kitchen and glanced in the living room, checking behind the couch. The house was quiet. I went downstairs to check his studio, looking in behind doors as I went, in case he'd passed out, fallen over, and hit his head.

I didn't open the door to the basement storage room. It was the one place in the house I didn't look.

I stood in his studio for a while, thinking. On his easel was the Great White Heron painting he'd been working on. That morning I noticed the sky. Was it different now, or had I just noticed it? An ominous black storm was coming, in the distance, reaching across the sky with thin fingers, so that even the elegance of the white birds in the foreground was now over-shadowed by what loomed in the distance. The storm dominated the paint-ing, threatened the creatures crouching vulnerable in the open swampland.

I could see that the painting was not about the birds; the painting was about the storm coming. There are three herons crouching in the marshland, hiding in the reeds as best they can. Two of them stare back at the storm thundering nearer and nearer. They bear down as it approaches.

But the other bird faces away from the storm, in the other direction, to where the sky is still light, poised.

Is that bird about to fly from the storm?

But the painting wasn't finished. When he finished a painting, he always signed it, and it wasn't signed.

"Jim?" I said quietly, as if I could feel him there.

I wondered then about his bedroom upstairs. My parents' house was three stories tall, with the top floor looking down from a wraparound balcony to the main floor. When I came out of the basement and turned to the foyer, I noticed the room was filled with a strange yellow light; more a glow than a light, actually.

I turned to look up to the bedrooms; I could see that the light was concentrated in a wide beam, maybe like a pillar, reaching two stories, from the roof to the floor. It was as if the sun was shining through a skylight, but there was no skylight, not there. It was a beam of soft light stretching to the floor in front of my feet. It filled me with a gentle sense of calm.

I can't tell you why this happened or even what it meant to me at the time; I can only tell you that I walked carefully around this beam of light and knew not to walk through it. It shone on to the floor at the edge of the staircase, so I could still climb the stairs to the bedrooms without disturbing it, I moved through the house as if in a dream. But halfway up the stairs, the light grew more intense, as if it was too hot to be close to, but there was no heat coming from it.

I couldn't climb anymore stairs. It was as far as I could go with the beam there. I could hear singing, softly at first, voices like a choir, singing *Holy, Holy, Holy.*

The light glowed in a way that made me feel exposed and ashamed for watching it, as if I had walked in and disturbed what was happening there. I had to look away from it to get my balance. I lay there on the stairs and watched the light pulsing at the edges.

I found myself singing then with the voices, *Holy, holy, holy, merciful and mighty. . . .*

Then the voices stopped and the light was gone, as if it had been switched off, quite suddenly, just like that. But I was still singing, to myself now, it seemed. The room and the staircase were as ordinary as they had been any other day. I climbed the stairs and checked the bedrooms for my brother, but he wasn't there.

It'll be okay, I thought.

I locked the door behind me and went back to work.

The day felt strange. I stayed in my office and ate a sandwich staring out the window at the liquor store, hoping to catch a glimpse of my brother. I wasn't angry anymore.

By two o'clock I knew I shouldn't be there. I should go home, I thought.

I drove to Canadian Tire to see James during his afternoon coffee break, as I sometimes did. The store was the same as it would have been any other day. I walked to the staircase at the back of the store, pulled the heavy door open, and started up.

James was already at the top of the stairs when I began to climb.

How did he know I was coming?

Then everything slowed down.

James was there.

At the top.

Staring down at me.

He looked scared.

His mouth was moving but I couldn't hear him.

I could see him rushing down the stairs toward me in slow motion.

I stopped on the stairs and watched him, so upset and frightened looking.

What on earth was he saying?

My ears had twisted themselves shut; they couldn't hear the words, they closed so tightly I had to blink and shake my head to begin to hear anything at all.

"He shot himself," he said.

Who did? I wondered. Who had shot himself?

"Jimmy!"

I imagined, at that moment, a bullet hole in his foot, broken bones and blood, probably a cast and more hospital visits, probably drinking. It would be another difficult day.

"He shot himself, Heather."

"How did you know I was coming?" I said.

"Your work called. Heather, he shot himself."

Then Linda Steadman appeared at the top of the stairs with her purse and her coat partway on.

She stopped and looked down the stairs at me.

"Oh my God, Heather," she said. "I just can't believe it."

What can't she believe? I wondered.

It must be a serious wound, I thought; it must be bad.

"Let's go," Linda said to us then. "I'll drive you."

She was coming with us.

She was offering to drive. Why would she do that?

"Is he okay?" I asked.

"I don't think so," she said.

She didn't say what she already knew was true.

"What do you mean, you don't think so?" I said. "What do you mean? What did they say? Where is he?"

"At your dad's," she said.

I started to run for the car.

"Do you want me to drive?" she asked.

"No!" I snapped.

It was the very last thing in the world I wanted.

I wanted everyone to get out of my way so I could get us there.

Now. Right now.

If he was seriously injured, he could be hanging on to the corner of his life with a tiny thread, and everyone had better get out of my way.

Most people did not understand my brother, I thought.

As I drove I began to realize they thought Jimmy was dead.

James and Linda actually thought he was dead.

Who would say such a thing?

They'd better do nothing until I get there, I thought.

They'd all better do nothing until I get there.

He might look dead but people don't understand my brother; they don't know all the details.

He's not dead.

"He might not be dead at all, you know!" I said then, scolding them, my foot to the floor. Faster, you hopeless car! I had to get to him; I had to get there before somebody did something stupid.

When I reached our house, I stopped the car on the road because there were four other cars in our driveway. Aunt Pat's car was there, and other cars, blocking up the driveway, at a time like this!

My dad's truck was home; why was he home? He was supposed to be away for work.

I ran for the door.

There were people sitting at our kitchen table; strange people who shouldn't be there.

Pastor Phil was there.

Why would Pastor Phil be here? Didn't he know this was a crisis?

Why wouldn't these people go away at a time like this? Did no one tell them?

Where was Jimmy?

Where the fuck was my brother?

"What's happened?" I yelled at them.

Pastor Phil shook his head and looked sad.

"Where's my dad?" I said. "Where is my father?"

"He's out at the picnic table, outside." My Aunt Pat looked white.

"Where's Jimmy?" I said.

"He's downstairs," someone said.

I turned and ran for the stairs.

Someone should be helping him, for God's sake, not just sitting there doing nothing! Imagine them all just sitting there doing nothing while he was probably bleeding! Imagine that!

At the bottom of the stairs I could see the door to the storage room had been left open and the lights were on inside.

I came around the corner and saw his legs then and the shotgun in his hands on top of his chest. I could not see his face. I stood above his body and was too confused to understand it.

Why was there a black garbage bag on his head, I wondered? He won't be able to breathe with that on his face.

Blood had leaked out of the bag and had pooled on the floor.

I only really understood what was happening when I looked down and saw James on the floor, holding his body, hugging on to Jimmy's legs, wailing.

"Jimmy! Oh, my God, Jimmy!"

He was crying, holding my brother's legs, sobbing, his head hugging Jimmy's chest.

I bent down too.

This was . . . Jimmy?

I lifted the edge of the bag to see his face.

It was him.

He was dead.

I'd left him and he'd been all alone.

He'd faced this terrible moment alone, I thought.

He'd been completely alone.

It was all I could think.

He'd had to pull that trigger himself, alone.

My God, he must have been so scared. And I'd left him alone.

Beside him on the floor, he had propped a miniature painting he'd done a couple of years ago. It was a painting I'd seen a hundred times but hadn't taken notice of it really. It was a grassy field with a storm coming, a simple tombstone as the focus, inscribed RIP.

Rest in Peace.

I don't know how long we stayed there in the basement, but when we got to the top of the stairs, I knew what I needed to do.

I called everyone together to do the only thing I could think of to do.

Yes, I was out of my mind, but no one argued or questioned me. They wouldn't have dared, not with the way I was moving about the house.

I took charge, having just left my brother in the basement in a pool of his own blood.

"Come in here, everyone," I said to the people gathered around the house, at the table, leaning on the backs of couches, coming in the back door, faceless people, a crowd of strangers carrying casserole dishes who didn't know my brother from a hill of beans, but if they were here in the middle of all of this, well they'd need to participate, get on and do what needed doing. They must have thought I'd lost my mind.

"Come in here and join hands," I said, gathering us in a circle in the foyer, where the pillar of light had shone through to the floor that morning.

No one argued with me.

The people from the kitchen and the living room trickled over slowly to stand with me in the circle—Pastor Phil, Aunt Pat, James, Linda Steadman, others whose faces I can't see now, stood together holding hands.

No one but me knew why we stood in that place, in a circle around the very place where, that morning, a strange light had shone.

I closed my eyes and spoke in a loud voice to God, to the Universe, to everything in the sky that would listen, in a voice that felt like it belonged to someone else.

"God of Light, Creator of the Universe," I said loudly and in my mind I could see the sun and the moon and the stars gathering too. It was not the way I normally prayed, but that day there were no rules to follow; that day I was free.

"We ask you to be with him, to take care of him. Take him safely, stay beside him the whole way so that he's not alone. Please don't leave his side until he gets there. Tell him we love him. Amen."

When I opened my eyes, I couldn't tell anyone why we'd had to stand there, how that morning the beam of light had reached through the ceiling and through the floor, like some kind of portal to another place. We stood in a circle around the place the light had shone, directly above his body, still lying in the storage room in the basement below us. I knew then that the light had not just shone from the ceiling to the living room floor—that was only the section I got to see, the section I dared not disturb when I crept up the stairs.

The beam had reached from somewhere out in the Universe, right through the house and into the basement below. The light had come from somewhere far away, and had found him there, at the moment he was most alone.

Jimmy would never finish the painting he'd left propped on his easel, the herons crouching, the storm approaching on the horizon. Days later, when the police had gone and had scrubbed the blood from the floor as best they could, I wanted to be in his studio again. I wanted to look at his things, his paintbrushes, the grey water he'd used that last day.

I held my breath when I looked at the painting on the easel, half expecting that third heron, the one that was poised to fly off toward the light, to be gone too.

But the painting was the same.

There we were, still, the three of us.

The casket was closed for the funeral, but the family was invited to view the body the night before. They'd dressed Jimmy in a plaid flannel shirt. Was it my mother's choice? She'd arrived home just before the funeral. It was a good choice, what he would have chosen himself for such a day.

It was a beautiful summer evening, so the dim little viewing hall felt stuffy and crowded, even with just a few people filing in past the body, uncles and aunts and cousins, the silence of the room being broken occasionally with a sudden sob, me holding out tissues at the exit, directing them to the smoking area outside where they all stood afterward, shaking, smoking, dabbing their eyes. I didn't cry.

Afterward, when they'd all gone, I breathed easier.

"I'll wait in the hall," James said, giving me time alone.

So there we were, one last time, my brother and me, in the quiet.

"They should have put your glasses on," I said to him. They were in his hand so I slid them onto his face. They'd done their best to rebuild the bridge of his nose and his forehead, but it had begun to collapse. I slid my fingers softly across the skin that covered his skull, touching the little bumps that protruded from the inside, where the pellets had embedded themselves in the bone. Makeup couldn't do much about that.

"You did a good job of that," I said to him, sighing, shaking my head, feeling the bumps, memorizing them with my fingers. He had a paintbrush in his other hand. That was a nice touch, I thought.

I didn't bend to kiss him the way my aunts had. Instead I closed my eyes and held my hand on his chest, feeling the white button of his shirt beneath it, feeling every moment we'd lived together.

And when I was finished, I closed the lid slowly and turned the latch to secure it. He was gone.

33

fterward is a place.

It's the still grey room you find yourself in, breathing, willing the curtains to never open again, longing for the glow of the sun at the edges to fade into night. In that room every window in every direction looks toward the moments of that last day, counting how long it's been, how much time has passed, every dawn and every dusk hanging over that singular reference point by which the whole of life was now measured.

The day my brother died, the earth split open at my feet, tearing the crust of the planet wide into a dark cavern at my toes. I stood on the edge, peering down, incredulous.

Afterward, I gripped on to whatever I could reach, whatever branch I could grab hold of without moving. I found myself trembling at the edge of this burnt forest, the fire officially out. I could see the path the fire had travelled, destroying everything green in its wake, as if nothing green would ever grow there again, as if the soil had been cursed. We walked through this new world to which we'd been banished, day after day after day, moving silent as ghosts, stepping over logs, going out only when there was no way to stay in, our faces covered in grief like charcoal, the ashes marking us, inviting the sympathetic smiles of people who had no idea what to say. What was there to say?

In the way I once carried stones from the lake to mark the earth, in this same way I felt there was something that must be *done*. Perhaps more balanced people come across such a burnt forest and step through until they reach the other side, but the sense that there was something that must be done would not leave me.

And then, as deep calls to deep, I knew what to do.

Was it madness?

In my mind I dug into the charred earth with my bare hands as if planting a tree: one small tree that would live. I held my breath, visioning the forest that would grow, that could live through such a thing, a forest that would begin again with one tiny tree, the first sign of life.

And when she was born, we named her Amelia Elizabeth. I could not take my eyes from her; she was the sun and the moon and the stars wrapped in soft pink skin. She was proof that life would begin again. Occasionally, an entire day would pass and I would notice, stunned, that I hadn't thought of Jimmy once that day. I knew then, I was truly beginning to lose him. I cried in the bath.

Afterward, I went back to study and books and theology, holding on for dear life to something I knew the feel of in my hand. When our son was born, I read theology texts with him on my chest, our wonderful boy, Jonathan James, snuggled into my neck, our daughter already singing and spinning in pretty dresses. I prayed when they slept, feeling their tiny puffs of breath on my cheek. I prayed that I would know how they needed to be loved, and that I could love them this way. I wrote papers and prepared for exams, but I could no longer remember why.

And then one day, perhaps because I was finally ready, all the pieces of this long journey, all the fragments of my life, came rushing together, like iron shavings drawn by a magnet. In one moment, the shreds of what I believed in, the remnants of truth I had salvaged, would be gathered the way a tornado gathers debris; the slender tip of the funnel touching down on the earth—in that one place, on that one day—would change everything.

The restaurant was quiet that morning; the kids were at home with James so I could work. It was so quiet I was easily distracted from my reading by the crinkle of wrappers from the small family of five nestled across the aisle from me, nibbling on hash browns, talking quietly among themselves, all church-tidy in skirts and pressed shirts, the littlest one with ribbons to match her dress.

The door must have opened without me noticing. I didn't even see the man come in. I was busy reading, enjoying a pleasant McCoffee, working on a paper about the Church and Mission.

There was suddenly shouting: a large man, much taller than 6 feet and easily 250 pounds, yelling, hollering at the top of his voice, shouting through a bushy black beard, angry and distressed.

He was a giant in a silver-studded, leather biker vest, his arms were covered in tattoos of snakes and demons, so many tattoos they were all I noticed at first.

At first, I didn't even see the white cane.

He was swearing, yelling, *someonefuckenhelpme, goddamnit,* whipping his cane against the plastic seats, wielding it like a machete, cutting a violent path through a nightmare, coming straight at us down the aisle.

Everyone in the restaurant was still.

He wore dark glasses so I couldn't see his eyes, but he swung his head from side to side like a bear that had been shot.

He stank so much I could smell him from ten feet away.

Booze, cigarettes, dirty clothes.

Spitting and shouting, cussing and stomping, *someonefuckenhelpme.*

It was only when I slowed that moment down later, that I heard the words the way I wish I'd heard them that day: *For Christ's sake—someone help me.*

I was frightened all right—frightened for my life. But he was blind so I hoped he couldn't sense me there. I was still, breathing carefully, hiding like a bird in a nest, praying he'd pass me by. His cane swiped a tray from a table, sent it crashing to the floor. He didn't stop; he passed right by like a cold wind taking down trees. Then he disappeared down the restroom hallway.

Across from me the mother whispered to her children. She crumpled up the wrappers, motioned to the little one to pick up her Barbie. The father stood, tucked his Bible under his arm, and moved into the aisle, keeping an eye out. The mother buttoned up her peach cardigan and waved them toward the door. Hurry.

The blind man had disappeared down the hallway, but he was making a terrible noise, banging and shouting, *goddamnsomeonefuckenhelp!*

The family and I—from the *good* people of the world, there in the restaurant, safe and happy, well groomed, dressed a little sharper than others on that Sunday morning—we exchanged glances.

Then a very small thing happened.

So small you could easily miss it.

The father smiled flatly at me, shaking his head to indicate a kind of pity, raising his eyebrows, inviting me to smile back.

The worst part is—I did.

I smiled right back at him, accepting his gesture with a slight turn-up of my lips and a nearly invisible nod. How the same we were, he and I; how good we were and what good choices we'd made. *Some people just can't be helped*—smile.

And just like that, we were safe inside our own gated world, slipping in behind some invisible wall to keep out the darkness that frightened us. We agreed about many things in our small exchange. *Everybody makes choices. Sometimes all you can do is pray.* Under different circumstances we might have even introduced ourselves. Good-bye.

The blind man was still in the hallway.

I couldn't see him but I could hear him.

Everyone could.

The whole restaurant stank of him.

The father held the door open for the mother. The children ran across the parking lot to the silver Land Rover. And then I remembered. It hadn't even occurred to me until that moment.

I'd forgotten the locked door.

And the sign: "Washrooms under renovation. Ask for key to Staff Washroom at front counter."

The blind man had stopped kicking the door but he still cried out, *forchristsake.*

By the time I got to him with the key, stumbling over my feet and my words, I couldn't breathe. He was sobbing. His pants were wet. A puddle of urine surrounded his shoes, but he was blind so I pretended I couldn't see what had happened.

"I'll get the door open for you," I said to him. Only a universe too late.

I'm sorry. Please forgive me, I wanted to say. But I didn't dare ask him then to squander his forgiveness on me.

Instead, I touched his shoulder and turned him toward the unlocked door but there was a dying, sorry part in me that needed to say more to him. Trembling, I reached for his hand; I touched his skin and felt the human heat between us. I expected him to flinch but he didn't. I placed his hand gently on the door handle but touched him for a moment more.

And a moment more.

He allowed me this secret repentance.

We didn't speak.

He disappeared into the bathroom, and I never saw him again.

For the first time in years, the fog lifted and I could see: How could a human malfunction quite so completely so the world is left crying, in a puddle of its own urine? How could I know the road to Jericho story in the marrow of my bones and yet turn up quite so smiling Sunday foolish?

That night I didn't sleep. A strange shivery sensation hummed inside of me while I waited for the night to pass. I lay awake thinking: awake with the man in the restroom hallway, the puddle of urine at his feet; awake with Bruce on the bench on George Street, with Charlie and the

Christian Life Centre; awake with Tiffany and the doll with the purple marker on her face. I lay awake with Jimmy.

In the morning, the glow of the sun at the edge of the curtains called to me.

It was time; something had changed in me.

I threw open the drapes, not just because the night was over, but because a new day had begun. The sun filled the room. I called the university to withdraw from the Bachelor of Theological Studies.

A woman answered the phone at St. Marks.

"I need to complete the paperwork at our end," she said. "What's your reason for withdrawing?"

I was quiet for a long time, thinking.

What I wanted to say to her was that there had to be a better way to do this, there had to be a better way to be a human being.

Instead I told her I'd get back to her.

I haven't yet.

It would be years before I understood what happened inside of me that day. It was not until my father was in a hospice, dying, that I would finally understand.

34

The nurses who visited my father were not chaplains, but they'd mastered the *ministry of presence* perhaps without knowing it. At St. John's Theological College, I'd studied with a peace-filled man who had been a chaplain for thirty years. He was gentle, patient, wise.

I envied him. I was young and fiery in the early years of theological school. If the chaplain was a gentle bed of hot coals that would keep watch through the night, I was a blaze of flame and smoke. Chaplains are called to the ministry of presence, which for me had been a nearly insurmountable challenge.

But when my father was dying, I began to settle in, in the most natural way, and for the first time in my life I found myself able to sit at the edge of this sacred calling and rest beside him. The ministry of presence is about accompanying someone on their journey, especially at their darkest moments. It's about being present in the midst of another's dark night. I have great difficulty with this; I am one who must do something, fix something, act, run, race, help.

But the world needs chaplains; people who carry the ministry of presence with them always; people who can share the journey of another's dark night, who can hold the most vulnerable of life's moments in their bare hands. As my father began to disappear from this life, this was what he needed more than anything else.

When I first learned to drive, a stray dog with the brightest button eyes had been hanging around our yard. Jimmy had been feeding it table scraps. One afternoon it ran out in front of my car and disappeared before I heard the thump. Jimmy watched it happen from the front lawn.

I heard the squealing and yelping and I froze. I couldn't get out of the car.

Jim was running, shouting, "Roll the car back! Roll the goddamn car back!"

The yelping was deafening; I couldn't think.

"Roll the car back!" he yelled.

I was shaking, but I rolled it back slowly.

He took off his shirt, and bent to the dog. He wrapped the dog in his shirt and held it close to his chest while we drove to the veterinary hospital. The dog's tail had been severed so Jimmy held the tail in his hand as we drove.

Yes, in his hand.

I don't think I could have done that. I don't know if I could have gotten out of the car if he'd not been there. I just don't know.

This is how it felt when I was with my father sometimes, especially while we were still at home. I woke up at night to see him there in his chair, alone in the dark.

"Do you want to talk for awhile?" he'd say, softly begging me to be with him, his wife finally resting, exhausted.

"Sure," I'd say, praying for the grace I needed to hold the tail.

This is the ministry of presence.

Through those long nights I often thought of Jimmy.

Could I manage it now? Could I be the sister who would take that broken boy in her arms and hold him, not noticing he might not make it? Could I stay with him through the night that might never end?

I pray for the grace to be this person.

The most precious thing my father left me was his fishing tackle box filled with a lifetime of treasures: hooks and shiny lures, spools of line, hand-tied flies his own father had left for him, but also new hi-tech gadgets he'd ordered online and never had a chance to try out.

"Sit down here and let's go through this," he said one afternoon, when he was alert and thinking, dragging the tackle box close enough to open it wide from his chair and pull out the hi-tech package he'd been studying for several months. It was complicated.

"Pay attention now," he'd said, not scolding me but certain if I didn't focus I would never get the damn thing right.

I'm not a serious fisherwoman; I'm more the easy-going, sunny day with a picnic and a fishing rod type. I think this is what made him read the directions out loud—all of them—and dangle the lures to mimic the motion to be looking for in the water.

"It should be slow like this, not any faster. Do you understand?"

I did, I told him.

"Now you need to go online and watch the video about it. I've written the address here on the back for you. Can you read that? Don't forget, now. Watch it before you try it out or you'll tangle it all up."

He was shaking his head as he folded it back up neatly, his hands trembling. He could tell I wasn't paying attention to the details as much as he wished I would.

But I could not. I was weeping inside myself, willing the tears to run down the insides of my eyes so that he wouldn't see me. There was my father in his chair, wanting to make sure I got this right, as if he was going away on a trip, and I'd need to look after things. He was passing on what he'd learned across the years, trying to store all of that wisdom somewhere safely in his daughter's mind. I listened to him teaching me to sharpen the hooks, to tie on the weights, and to store the small boxes in the bottom of the tackle box this way—turn them this way *only*—and I prayed I would remember the sound of his voice always.

For as long as I can remember, in the autumn I have gone to see the salmon coming upstream. When I had children of my own, I often thought of my father and how patient he was to explain this miraculous event. At the end of their lives, salmon return to the stream of their birth to die. I wonder if they know this is happening? I wonder when it occurs to them—*it's time?*

Perhaps they are swimming along in the ocean, after a lifetime of strong and silvery leaps into the sky, when it suddenly occurs to them—*it's time.* But when they arrive at the edge of the stream from which they came, do they feel the fresh water spilling out into the ocean and remember? Do they hesitate then, at the edge, circling, darting away into the deep perhaps, knowing they will enter the stream to die? Do they long for one last wide open run through the sea before it's over? Do they arrive alone?

Together, the salmon who have come to die make their way inland, their red bodies thumping and scraping on the rocks in a few inches of water while they push on, their flesh tearing off in chunks, until they can swim no further and their bodies lie lifeless on the edge of the water.

Dying is hard.

When we can no longer look after him safely at home, when he falls in the bathroom a second time, we ask my father if he is ready to go into hospice.

He darts at the edge of the stream, circling, sleeping more, moving less, growing thinner.

Then one afternoon, he says it. "I guess it's time."

He begins the journey upstream.

I say things like, this will be good, Dad, we can get outside there and go for walks.

We both pretend it will be great.

The hospice is a beautiful and tragic place, a warm gathering of people who have come to die. When I walk the halls in the morning, I notice new rooms that have become vacant in the night, the visitors gone, the bed stripped and the floor scrubbed. In the foyer of the hospice stands a stately looking grandfather clock. When it's quiet you can hear the bells chime from the far end of the hall.

For years I've wondered about bells. A bell maker on Salt Spring Island once told me that human beings resonate inside with the vibration of bells, and that perhaps we are healed by this resonance passing through our bodies. I smiled and nodded at the time, dubious. But that afternoon, when I stood next to the bells hanging up in his old shed and felt their music shuddering up inside my spine, I dared to wonder if he might be right.

Could it be? Could there be some mystical healing brought on by the sound of bells?

On the Saturday before my father died, we took him out in the wheelchair for a morning walk. I pushed the chair, and Dona and my cousin Lorri navigated the puddles. We filled the trail with chatter and laughter, carrying on as if my father was not silent, not confused, not disappearing. The sun was warm, the birds flitted in the trees nearby, and the pussy willows looked as if they might nearly be ready, longing to feel the sun on their faces as much as we did.

But when we finally made it back to the front door, I looked at my watch and realized we were late. We'd missed his meds and lunch delivery and the doctor. So I began to push him faster, rushing him back to the schedule, hurrying him around the corner when my father, who had not spoken all day, called out in a loud voice:

"Stop!" he said.

It startled me.

But then I realized what he wanted.

It was noon.

The grandfather clock was chiming, sounding out the measured moments of that last golden morning.

Others had stopped too. And there they were—the dying—gathered near the clock, listening, as if in some sacred space, the deep resonance of the bells passing through their broken bodies was calling to them from across the years. These simple, beautiful moments: the treasure of the dying.

At the hospice a nurse told me that people who are dying like to be touched; in fact need to be touched. And so I began to do that, when it seemed like my father was slipping away, disappearing into the land of the dying too soon, I would reach over and rub his arm or hold his hand for a while, something I may not have done when he was well.

When I touched him, when I felt his skin underneath my fingertips, I could see his whole body ease a little, reflecting a kind of warmth that I, too, felt inside of myself. And I began then to think about *touch*. The word *touch*, said my Google search, reaches back to the ancient Latin *toccare* meaning to "strike a bell." To strike a bell.

And isn't this the way it is? When we, in the land of the living, are touched by someone, when we are deeply connected as human beings, when someone has *touched* us, stepped inside that shivery, paper-thin layer, it's as if a bell has been struck whose deep vibrations awaken us from the inside, disrupting the silence, throwing open the curtains and letting in the morning light.

And there in the hospice room as my father slept, I began to think about that Sunday morning with the blind man in the restroom hallway. And I knew then, what happened that day.

When I'd touched that lonely man, when I felt the warmth of his skin under my fingertips, for one brief moment, that touch, that *toccare*—that strike of the bell—began to resonate inside of me, passing through my body with some kind of mysterious healing, the scales falling from my eyes so that I might see.

This was my healing.

Thou restoreth my soul. My cup runneth over.

Why was I so surprised?

35

My father's eyes are mostly closed now. There will be no more walks outside; no more racing through the puddles in his wheelchair. When he wakes, the sparkling brown of his eyes, now ringed with a cloudy blue, are the color of confusion.

He scans the room, searching our faces, wanting to recognize someone—anyone. Who are you, he asks with his eyes. He doesn't say the words; he just stares.

"You're okay, Dad," I say. "You're okay."

I am praying he doesn't feel afraid; I whisper in his ear, bless him with the peace that passes all understanding. He is deep beneath purple layers of consciousness, not able to lift his head above the water.

I stroke his arm, memorizing the feel of his hand in mine.

"I'm here," I say to him.

He closes his eyes and slips beneath the water again.

I hold my breath and squeeze his hand; even with his eyes closed, he squeezes back, holding on tight.

Yesterday, Lance arrived.

Is it too late?

Lance. Jimmy's best friend, a son to my father. He's flown in from San Francisco. I wish for my father a moment of lucidity, to feel the love for him in the room. The faces from my childhood have come; from the

214

days of my father's strong hands, his four-wheel-drive truck, his pipe wrenches.

Visitors whisper in the chair beside his bed, taking turns sitting with him as he sleeps. If he could feel how loved he is for one moment; one moment would be enough. Is love one of the things we can take with us at the end?

None of us knew how fast this disappearance would come, blowing in like a strong wind across the water—as if out of nowhere.

My father sleeps.

Lance is the bearer of music, of laughter, of a thousand memories of sing-a-longs by the piano. How have we arrived here, so far from the land of our childhood?

"I've arranged for you to play the piano in the hospice lounge," I'd said to him on the phone, just days before, grasping for a way to conjure up the magic of years already spent.

"Bring your music!" I'd said with a little too much invested in it.

And of course he does. Lance brings his music. At the time I imagined laughter and rousing Billy Joel lyrics thumping from the piano, all of us together, stomping up a few good choruses, one last time.

But this morning, my father is deep underneath, in a muted world of his own. Even when I reach for him, he's not strong enough to reach back. How is it this happened so quickly?

And then—when I resign myself to the truth that he will probably not leave his bed again—he brightens. He asks to sit up a little; his eyes focus; he smiles at us all in the room.

"Holy moly," he says, surprised to see us all there, taking it all in. He smiles and rests his head back, not to sleep, but to take it all in.

"We're all here," I say to him. He nods and smiles, understanding. People talk, he responds, even throws out a joke or two. He has come up, lifted his head from the silent purple world. When I see he is truly with us, awake in a way I haven't seen for days, I ask him gently: "We were thinking you might like to hear a few songs on the piano. Would you like that, or would you rather rest?"

"I'd like that," he says. But I'm not sure he means it, so I let him sit for a while and then ask again. "Do you think you'd like to hear some music?"

"Of course," he says, a little annoyed at why I didn't pay attention the first time.

I'm not sure he's strong enough to even sit in the wheelchair, but he wants to try. The nurses come to help him. It takes all his strength just to be moved from the bed. I second-guess myself. Is this my own selfishness, wanting him to be with us as he used to be? His eyes are clouded, he breathes heavily, he shivers. *Is he doing this for me?*

I wheel him slowly down the hallway to the lounge. Lance is already there with my cousin Lorri and her husband, Brian. Mostly my father is busy blinking, taking in the new surroundings. His hands shake. He's not distressed but confused.

This was probably a mistake.

"Where would you like me to park you?" I say to him, gently.

He points to a corner across from the piano. I'm not sure he knows where he is.

Then, because we're here now and no matter what, we'll have to make the best of it, Lance fires up the grand piano, the energy and life of a thousand memories delivered in every note.

And I see then, what I know I was longing for: my father's smile.

The music fills the room.

Lance sings. His voice calms my father.

He taps his fingers to the music and smiles.

Lorri and I chime in awkwardly with the few lyrics we remember, but Billy Joel lights the place up. I join Lance to stand by the piano and watch for my father's eyes. The joy of music fills us all. I pretend I'm not crying, hoping my father can't see. I keep singing because we're all here, we're present together in this music as we will never be again. In my mind, Jimmy is there with us, singing along, just like old times.

Sing us a song you're the Piano Man. . . .

Then I see it.

He's crying. I rush to him and crouch by his chair.

"Is this too much? Do you want to go back?" I say to him.

What have I done?

"No, no . . ." he shakes his head, his tears are somehow happy, sacred even.

He is with us in the midst of this music, fully alive on the earth.

"Are you okay?" I ask him.

He nods.

Sing us a song tonight . . .

My father weeps, but he's smiling.

He is aware now that this moment is a gift. That he is dying. That this is a treasure we will never share again.

Cause we're all in the mood for a memory. . . .

He looks down at me crouching beside his chair, looking up into his face. Even though I know I should, I can't stop myself from crying. The music is loud and fills the space.

Then he says to me the words I will remember forever:

"I don't suppose . . ." he says with a twinkle in his eye, "you'd care to dance?" He smiles, tilts his head to the side, with a strange mix of sorrow and joy, knowing it's impossible.

"Dad," I say, "if I could, I would dance with you forever."

So because we cannot dance, I lay my head on his lap like a child and feel the music in the room. He pats my head and lets me cry.

"This is a hard one to take, isn't it?" he says then, tears flowing like a mountain spring.

"It sure is," I say, falling underneath the spell of the music, seeking the strength of my father for this one last moment, drinking in the comfort he offers me.

The music plays on, and we swim in the memories.

Dancing, if only in our minds, and singing as if there was no tomorrow.

36

The night before the celebration of my father's life, we held a small prayer service in the little church by the ski hill. All these years later, though it had changed denominations several times, the building was still a church. When I explained to the caretaker that my father had helped to build the church many years ago, that he'd dug the ground and poured the cement and hammered in the nails that held it there, he agreed to let us use it for the service.

"Just stop by and get the key," he'd said.

The key.

How had so many years passed?

I held it in my hand like a treasure.

When the key turned in the door, my heart pounded in my chest.

I climbed the stairs.

The velvet curtain was no longer there, but when I stood inside the sanctuary, I felt I'd come home. At the front of the church was the same wide wooden altar carved with the words: "Do this in remembrance of me."

My fingers traced the smooth edges of the letters and I remembered and remembered.

We lit the window ledges with candles that night, so the little church by the ski hill glowed like a lantern, as if fireflies lit the sanctuary.

218

Fireflies. They carry within their tiny insect bodies the ability to *be* light in a dark world. Could this somehow be true for us too? Fireflies flash to communicate with one another in a language science doesn't yet understand. In some species of fireflies, even their tiny eggs glow, long before they know they're fireflies, before they've become the creatures they hope to be; the glow inside of them is present right from the beginning, even before they know what to do with it. Perhaps this is true for us all. Perhaps we are born with that light, carrying it inside of us long before we know what to do with it.

The pews in that tiny church were filled with the searching, hopeful faces of family and friends. They could not know what it meant for me to be standing there that night, in the church my father built, beside the husband I loved; they could not know how it felt that night, after such a journey, to stand in the place I once stood—to have found my way home.

From the moon you can see the Earth half lit up, like an intricate Christmas ornament with a loose wire: the world that's been unfolding for four-and-a-half billion years. I am four-and-a-half decades old as I write this. If instead, time was compressed and the Earth was my age, human beings would have been present on the planet for less than a month. And the Church would have shown up just nine minutes ago.

What made me think that the Earth, in all its flickering, mysterious wonder, should be colonized by the Church in nine minutes? I remember thinking, once, that it ought to be. What a strange way to think of this extraordinary, miraculous planet.

The Church will not contain God. God will never be "managed" that way. The Church is on a journey of its own. And this gives me hope. Perhaps it, too, will find light like the birch on Highland Drive, suddenly growing sideways, forcing a ninety-degree bend in the trunk before it springs up to clear the edge of the deck, breaking all the rules about the way trees are meant to grow.

My father passed away on Tuesday, March 5. That afternoon I had shared the gift of a quiet space with him in his room. He was agitated, uncomfortable, hadn't spoken since Sunday, could no longer eat or drink, breathing through the pain of shingles and the shadow of his own death.

His mind was confused, drifting in and out of consciousness. When he opened his eyes, they were wide and glassy.

I could see his fear.

All I could think of, all I could see written in his eyes, was the cry of Jesus from the cross: *Why have you forsaken me?*

Indeed. Perhaps the life that is given to us is mysterious on purpose. Perhaps what matters most is that we learn to live trying.

I opened the Prayer Book to read him Psalm 23.

The Lord is my shepherd; I shall not want.

He held my wrist, gripping on for dear life.

He makes me lie down in green pastures and leads me beside the still waters.

I stood beside his bed but read as if to the universe, as if my words could fill the sky.

When I finished the psalm, he was calm.

The waters were still and his grip softened.

Was this the end of the journey upstream, where the current was gentle?

He squeezed my hand tenderly, unable to speak.

Does he know who I am? I wondered. Does he know it's me?

His brown eyes were enormous, looking up at me without blinking, filled with expectation and longing, the way children look up during a story, waiting for the page to be turned, waiting to hear how it ends.

What next? I wondered. Where do you go from Psalm 23?

His eyes stared. He waited.

I flipped through the pages and found a liturgy for the dying.

Will he think I'm rushing him? No; the prayers, I could see, were beautiful and soothing, so I began.

God of mercy, receive him into your heavenly kingdom. Bless him and let him live with you forever.

He was smiling, listening to every word, tears were rolling down his cheeks as I read. He understood.

Have mercy on your servant. That it may please you to give him joy and gladness in your kingdom—with your saints in light.

Yes, I think. *With your saints in light.*

They will come for him.

Then there is a sound like the wind.

Is it only in my mind?

Something is coming.

At first when I see them in the distance, flashing and silver, reflecting the white light, I think, this must be it. This must be the shining wings of ten thousand angels.

Yes, I think, the saints in light, coming for my father.

But then I see.

The sound is not the wind, it is the water, the moon pulling hard from the sky, the sea itself rising up. The flashing is ten thousand salmon, strong and silvery, thrusting upstream, leaping and dancing in the light, scaling waterfalls as tall as trees, breaking all the rules on their way to somewhere new, listening to the voice of the One who calls them, their battered bodies shed and left behind on the shore.

"Good girl," my father said when I'd finished reading.

He squeezed my hand before he closed his eyes and slipped into a deep sleep from which he would not awake, making his way with the saints in light, following the stream deep into the forest that welcomed him home.

And somewhere in that forest, through every bright morning and every dark night, the circle of stones remains, marking the place on the earth that once held a family. And when the night is deep and lonely, as the night can often be, fireflies find that forest, bearing light.

Dear Reader,

Every 40 seconds someone in the world dies by suicide. More than 1 million people take their own lives every year. Mental illnesses are medical conditions that disrupt a person's thinking, feeling, mood, ability to relate to others, and daily functioning. Research shows that half of all mental illnesses start by age 14 and three-quarters start by age 24. Mental illnesses are treatable and hope for a brighter future is possible.

However, in Canada and the United States only 1 in 5 of these children is receiving appropriate treatment. The **Jim Young Fund for Mental Health** was created to make a difference.

I invite you to enjoy Jim's magnificent work as a wildlife artist by visiting his online gallery found in the "Jim Young Fund" on my website: www.heathergordon-young.com.

Prints of Jim's work are available for purchase online. All proceeds from the sale of these prints will go to the **Jim Young Fund for Mental Health** to support projects whose primary focus is mental health in rural and regional communities.

Please visit my website to enjoy photos from this true story and to view the Fireflies Backstory video. When you subscribe to my website by entering your email you will join other readers who wish to stay informed about future books and new releases of Jim's work.

With gratitude,

Heather Gordon-Young